WHAT IS CHRISTIANITY?

Unwrapping the Mystery,
which is Beyond
Simple Definition

Rev. M. Richardson

Rev. Dr. George Richardson

WHAT IS CHRISTIANITY?
Copyright © 2012 by Rev. George Richardson

Second edition published by Word Alive Press, 2012.

ISBN 978-1-77069-377-7

Word Alive Press
131 Cordite Road, Winnipeg, MB R3W 1S1
www.wordalivepress.ca

WORD ALIVE PRESS
Just Write!

Printed in Canada

MIX
Paper from
responsible sources
FSC   FSC® C016245
www.fsc.org

Library and Archives Canada Cataloguing in Publication

Richardson, George, 1924-
     What is Christianity? : unwrapping the mystery which is beyond simple definition / George Richardson.

ISBN 978-1-77069-377-7

     1. Christianity--Essence, genius, nature. 2. Bible--Criticism, interpretation, etc. 3. Theology, Doctrinal--Popular works. I. Title.

BT60.R53 2011   230   C2011-906313-1

This book is dedicated to our five daughters,
Gwendolyn, Joyce, Gloria, Ruth and Susan.

Table of Contents

Foreword   vii

Acknowledgements   xi

Introduction   xiii

    One: The Significance of Mystery   1

    Two: My Path to a Living Faith   23

    Three: The Bible, What It Is   37

    Four: The Influence of Other Cultures   59

    Five: Jesus of Nazareth   65

    Six: The First Christian Communities   75

    Seven: The Catholic Church   87

    Eight: The Protestant Reformation   101

    Nine: Expressing Beliefs   113

    Ten: A New Creed   119

    Eleven: Christianity Today   149

About the Author   153

Foreword

My eldest daughter Gwen raised the question "What is Christianity?" when she asked me to recommend a book that would tell her what Christianity is. Within a few weeks, my second daughter, Joyce, made the same request. Our five daughters are long past childhood and have become bright and lovely women. Conversation with them is one of the joys of my life and I would have liked to have responded with a title and author, but there are complications.

Christianity is not a static entity, but a dynamic movement that has been developing over a long time. Books purporting to set out what Christianity is are generally examples of how Christianity was thought of in a specific culture during a certain time period. Many of these books are well worth reading to broaden one's understanding of what Christians believed at the time when they were written. However, no one of these books could be recommended as setting forth the "correct" interpretation of Christianity.

In discussing this with Joyce, she suggested that I write a book. That put the matter in a different light. My daughters grew up in a home where Christianity was a constant influence and they deserve to have a thoughtful statement of my understanding of Christianity. Others who read these pages may be inspired to do some fresh thinking about religion in general and Christianity is particular.

I doubt that there is one "correct" interpretation of Christianity, so I cannot claim to present one, but I can share what I believe about God and my insights into what lies behind theories that have been used at various times in history to interpret Christianity. This will inevitably include my honest evaluation of these theories and may contribute to your thinking about the various types of Christianity you may be exposed to.

The most significant element in Christianity is the effect it can have on individuals and, through them, on their society. Put simply, Christianity is what happens in people when they believe that God who created everything has become known in Jesus Christ and make this the governing factor in their values, attitudes and actions.

The Bible provides records of what people remembered of Jesus. Their understandings give insight into the spirit in which Jesus lived and taught. That Spirit reveals God as loving each person, and intending that each care about others. Jesus taught by words and actions that every human life is sacred before God, even to those whom some people feel may not deserve it.

Jesus reveals God who wants each of us to care about, and care for, each human being we encounter. We discover the mystery of God within us when we constantly relate spiritually to God and feel prompted to a consistent caring about others. I call this living with God as Jesus did, and living for God in the spirit of Jesus' teaching and example.

Organized Christianity nourishes this with meeting together weekly to relate to God and help us think about and implement practical ways to help others.

Acknowledgements

I am grateful to the many people who have contributed to my appreciations of Christianity. Especially:

Dr. Donald Mathers, Systematic Theology Professor at Queen's University, who encouraged me to write my degree thesis on The Logic of Theological Language and who invited me to participate in a national committee of the United Church of Canada, which exposed me to the focused thinking of intelligent people from across the nation.

Dr. W.E.L. Smith, History Professor at Queen's University, who taught me to be aware of the role that ideas play within the thinking of the people of certain historical periods that influenced the course of their own history.

Church members in several congregations whose sharing of their feelings with me increased my awareness of what goes on in human souls.

Garfield Richardson, my father, who taught me to think logically in assessing the implications of public policies.

My adult children, whose conversation informs and stimulates my thinking. Especially Gwendolyn and Joyce, who encouraged me to write this book, and Ruth, who has been my contact with the publisher and a great help with the details involved.

My wife, Eunice, whose love has been a wonderful support in all my endeavours, including the writing of this book.

Introduction

This book encourages readers to use their intelligence to recognize a distinction between the packaging of Christianity and the reality that is revealed in the spirit of Jesus. It addresses the nature of the human soul, which is the point at which God interacts with the human individual. It offers the concept of soul dimensions to draw attention to factors you already know, but may not have given any thought to.

This book deals with the Bible, how it originated and developed over the centuries, and invites you to consider the circumstances under which parts of the Bible were written that influenced the writers' thinking about God and shaped the setting in which Jesus lived and taught.

It deals with Jesus' teaching; the reasons why he was opposed and eventually crucified; the mystery of the spirit of Jesus after the resurrection, and the way his followers developed theories to explain it; the Catholic Church; and the various types of reforms that produced numerous Protestant churches. It offers insights into the thinking behind *A New Creed* of the United Church of Canada.

This book encourages the reader to discover the way Christianity can enrich the soul's dimensions and transform the values of a society's culture.

CHAPTER ONE

The Significance of Mystery

You may enter a place of worship and be impressed by the architecture of a great cathedral or the simplicity of a small church. You may observe the words and attitude of the people there and the singing or rituals they may be engaged in. You may come away thinking you know what they were doing, but fail to grasp what is really going on, unless you recognize that these people come here to renew their sense of—and commitment to—a great mystery.

I realize the word mystery can be used to refer to that which is not known yet, as in mystery stories. Some may feel that calling something a mystery is way of making ignorance acceptable and avoiding the mental work of further investigation. I am not using the word for either of these purposes.

I speak of mystery to refer to that which can be known, but by its very nature cannot be seen, measured or localized. This mystery is a very real part of every person's life. To appreciate this mystery, think about what you mean when you say "I" in such statements as: I am happy. I am sad. I am angry. I am sorry. I am interested. I don't care.

What does "I" refer to? You know exactly what you mean when you use this term in such sentences. You are talking about an aspect of you that is very real, but is difficult to describe in precise words. It is obviously not any visible part of the body. It isn't your eyes, your ears, your elbow or your foot that loves, hates or makes decisions.

"I" is not your mind. Our minds process information we are receiving and can advise "I" about making decisions. It is very important to gather all the knowledge that is available, and equally important to think clearly about all the implications of that knowledge. Our minds can provide us with valuable insights to assist in making wise decisions.

However, "I" is not the mind. I can refuse to do what my mind tells me. My mind can tell me there is nothing to fear, yet I can still be afraid. My mind can tell me that I should act, but I can procrastinate. I can even muster my mind to justify decisions I have already made. My mind is obviously distinct from "I" and I am in charge.

There may well be emotions involved in dealing with a situation, but emotion is a different factor than "I". People have used the phrase "getting steamed up" as a way to describe someone getting emotional about something. This slang term is a useful metaphor for emotion. It comes from the days when steam engines were the main source of power. That power becomes available when water comes to a boil in a closed system. The resulting steam pressure can be released into a mechanism that turns wheels.

There was a period in history when applying steam power to transportation and manufacturing transformed a way of life for whole societies. However, steam pressure could also burst boilers with a destructive explosion, if not handled properly.

Emotion refers to generating passionate concern in the soul which can feed power into our loves and also into our resentments and fears. Like steam power, it can be a useful force which can give impetus to worthwhile initiatives but can explode with destructive consequences if not handled wisely.

"I" decides what thoughts I will entertain, what is important to me, what I value and what I will attempt. The many things that should be considered may be quite serious and sometimes emotional, but when all the input from every source is in, the power of decision rests with the mystery we refer to as "I."

We can look around and see the many items we use daily that make life more interesting and comfortable. If we think for a moment, we can recognize that each is available for us because someone (an "I") decided to produce it. The process of making such items available probably involved many people and much planning and organizing, but none of that could happen until there was first a decision made by someone (an "I" or a group of "I"s) who initiated the process.

Every aspect of economics, politics, clothing style and personal relationships depends on what individual persons decide in the mystery they refer to as "I". If enough "I"s decide to buy your product, your business will succeed. If they decide not to, your business will fail.

The advertising industry can be quite ingenious in devising ways to capture interest or emotion. A marketer's objective is to get minds or emotions to influence "I"s to make decisions that will be profitable for his or her purposes.

All of this indicates the tremendous power of mystery. We can't see, measure or locate what we mean by "I", but its mystery cannot be ignored as imaginary. Whatever word we use to refer to it, "I" is the most real thing in your life or mine. "I" makes the final decision about every issue, so it is worth giving thought to what we might know about the mystery of "I".

DIMENSIONS OF SOUL

For communication purposes, we call the reality we think of as "I" the soul or spirit. Science uses the Greek word psyche. We are thinking about the command centre of each individual's life. Because it is a mystery, we can't define exactly what any soul is. However, we can recognize that the soul may have several modes which act like dimensions, so I will use the concept of dimensions to think about "I".

A point has no dimensions, but stretching the point out in one direction makes it become a line with one dimension—think of a string. Spread the line sideways and it becomes a plane. Think of a sheet of paper that has two dimensions, length and width. Add a third dimension and think of a box. The box has length, width and height. Height does not eliminate the first two dimensions, but builds on them.

Having three dimensions does not tell you what is in the box, but the extent of those dimensions limits the nature of what the box can contain.

If you look for a box to hold things for the process of moving from one location to another, you will find that a long narrow box, such as is used for a fluorescent light, emphasizes one dimension and will not hold very much. A wide flat box, such as is used for pizza, emphasizes two dimensions and is not much better. But you can get more into a box that has a balance between its width and length and height. We can get a great deal more into our souls if they have several dimensions in balance.

I learned to think in terms of spiritual dimensions at a course in Pastoral Psychiatry. The original concept was from the work of David Hay, the former Director of the Religious Experience Research Institute in Oxford. His exploration of spiritual dimensions enables appreciation of the fact that that adding new dimensions does not negate the former dimensions, but rather enriches or expands them.

Life has more to it when lived in all its dimensions. The first dimensions of the soul are always there in a broader context. Without suggesting any limit to the number of possible dimensions one might consider, I will share with you seven dimensions that are significant to me.

1. SURVIVAL: The first dimension of the soul is our concern for the things we identify as necessary for survival. This is a basic dimension. A baby begins life with concern for food and comfort, but has limited abilities. A baby can only survive when there are one or more adults who take responsibility to provide for its needs. Each growing young person should learn how to obtain basic needs and how to handle situations to ensure supply.

Any philosophy of life that rejects this first dimension is unrealistic. A person who does not pay attention to economic and other needs will only survive if someone else provides for him or her. At every stage in life, the soul must continually pay attention to its economic base.

Primitive, one-dimensional religion often focuses on prayers and rituals intended to get God to change the way the world works, so that we may have our specific desires satisfied. Let us think about that for a minute.

Imagine that I have to work long hours cultivating a field and getting the soil loosened and black, with all vegetation covered, nicely prepared for seeds. I go to bed that evening intending to plant the seeds the next day. If the one-dimensional religion were true, I could awake the next morning to find that my field covered in luxurious grass! Someone else has prayed for pasture for horses.

Think what it would be like if God were to keep intervening whenever someone prayed, thereby changing the cause-and-effect pattern of nature in ways that would make any given cause have different results. Plans only work if there is some reliability in the situation. What we call science was only made possible after humans moved beyond that kind of religion and recognized that God has set up the world to be reliable.

This predictability enables our society to organize and make life more manageable. We are fortunate to live in a corner of the world where people have accomplished much by learning how God designed the world and applying that knowledge. I believe this is the way God expects humans to cope with life.

Relating to God serves a different purpose than our influencing God to break the laws of nature. It opens a channel through which God influences us, empowering us to be and to do what he created us for within his natural laws. There is real power in sensing the mystery of God as it can be seen in every situation, and consciously making whatever you do an offering for God in the spirit of Jesus.

Matthew's gospel says, *"Seek first his kingdom and his righteousness, and all these things shall be yours as well"* (Matthew 6:33).

Prayer for courage, hope, patience and power is realistic. God does give these gifts. I believe that going to

God with my concern about someone is bringing that person into the relationship I have with the mystery that is God, thereby contributing to the mystery that is the person I am praying for.

Engaging in verbal prayer with someone can help them to sense the presence of God and enter into a living relationship with God. Healing forces are strengthened, along with inflow of hope, patience and power. I have seen this happen in many times of crisis. I have come to trust this mystery, although it cannot be predicted.

I believe in miracles, but I don't believe that a miracle interferes with the cause-and-effect pattern which is built into the world. God enables us to endure or overcome the limits of our situations and may adjust the situation in ways that we haven't thought of. That is what I call a miracle.

Focusing on your own needs or desires can be a wholesome concern which leads you to make the best of your situation, but it can easily turn into narrowing life down to mere concern for accumulating stuff. It can lead to seeking what you want by shortcuts like theft or fraud. It can be expressed through hurting those we perceive to be hindering us from getting what we want, such as through unwelcome sexual advances or even rape.

The tendency for this first dimension to lead to destructive decisions does not mean that self-concern is wrong. This dimension is necessary, but needs to be balanced by higher dimensions and guided by a higher mystery.

I believe that faith in God is the awareness that everything we obtain for survival comes from a higher mystery working through various agencies. We should not only be thankful to God, but hold it all as a trust to be used for the purposes of God. This is treated in Jesus' parable of the talents in Matthew 25:24–30.

Christianity affirms that God in Christ loves us and calls us to care about others, including their need for survival. God loves them, too. God leads us to find solutions for our first-dimensional needs by earning our living through serving the needs of others.

My first occupation was farming, which produces food. The miracle of growth and reproduction provides food for all living things. One can farm with the awareness that respecting the fertility of the soil is a trust from God to ensure that God's design for feeding all types of life will continue. The daily tasks of planning and working the farm have a divine element, because one is sharing in the purpose of God.

There are many other ways by which one may earn a living through serving human needs. Medical doctors, nurses, and teachers come to mind, but there are many occupations in which the element of serving human needs can bring a divine purpose into daily tasks. This can influence a Christian's choice of a career and give meaning to the way it is pursued. Ways of making money that seek to take something from people without giving value in return are not Christian.

2. BELONGING: Every soul needs relationships with other souls. A baby begins life with a relationship to its mother that is built in, but the tiny soul has to develop a sense of belonging with its father and possibly siblings. Feeling belonging in a family unit is very significant for the development of the soul. When the growing young person moves beyond the family, he or she seeks belonging with some other group.

This is a very significant time in that young person's life. The soul's need for belonging is so important that those with whom the soul bonds can be very significant in the quality of the individual's life. Needing to belong can push them into helpful or destructive behaviour to meet the expectations of the group.

This second dimension can be a wholesome desire to relate to others and belong in their company. However, it can turn into an obsession and lead to submerging one's sense of self. A Christian sense of the sacredness of all human life includes the sacredness of one's own life. Jesus said, *"Love your neighbour as yourself"* (Mark 12:31). This blends respect for self with respect for others, so that belonging can be mutually supportive and encouraging, rather than manipulating any member of the group.

At any age it is very important to be wise in selecting the sort of group with whom you wish to belong. An ongoing relationship with God that feels the mystery of God with the mystery that is you protects you from desperate loneliness, which may lead you to make foolish choices. Christianity brings you into a church congregation, with opportunities to belong with people who are seeking relationship with God. Sharing with them in activities that serve human needs enriches the soul.

God made us for belonging in community, and the soul that does not find belonging with people is seriously deprived. A key factor in personal fulfillment is whether the mystery you think of as "I" is relating satisfactorily to similar mysteries in other people.

It is possible to deal with people as though they were merely a part of the general environment, seeing some as dangerous and others as available to be used. With this attitude, you can be awash in a sea of human beings, yet feel very alone. Have you ever noticed that the situation feels different when you recognize an individual person as an "I" that fears, loves, and has much they care about? Then you can relate to this mystery in a significant way, because you are a similar mystery.

The mystery of "I" is basic to who each of us is, making personal relationships interesting. By acknowledging this "I" and attempting to develop an acquaintance, we can know other people in a deeper way than words can describe.

Personal relationships neither have the exactness of mathematics nor the firmness of physics, but instead the dynamics of mystery. It is not something that can be handed to you like a book. You only keep a personal relationship by living it. You can't see belonging, but this dimension is a significant element of being human.

3. KNOWING: Knowing is an activity of the brain, but the "I" encourages or neglects it. This is first evident when a child asks, "Why?" He or she is expanding the soul's desire to know. Parental nurturing of a child's desire to know is very significant for the adult this child will become. The more one knows about anything, the better one can appreciate it and develop skills in dealing with it.

Society provides educational opportunities for children, but the whole educational system assumes that children have a desire to learn and depends on each child deciding he or she wants to learn. Teachers need to have faith in the mystery of each child and promote a desire to learn in the many "I"s in the classrooms.

Knowing and understanding enriches the first two dimensions. Knowledge makes you better able to provide for your needs or desires and guides your capacity to relate to people. University students need to find a satisfactory balance between attending to money matters, getting involved in social life, and seeking knowledge (the first three dimensions of the soul).

Knowledge can make life more interesting and productive in many ways, yet there is also the very real risk of assuming that what you know is all there is to know and closing your mind to further ideas. This is voluntary ignorance. It ignores the fact that the more one knows the better one can appreciate how much more there is to know.

Christianity includes knowledge about Jesus Christ. It includes becoming familiar with the stories Jesus told, the example of his dealing with people, and his teaching about God. This knowledge provides a basis for sensing his spirit and the mystery of his relationship with God.

Christianity makes you aware that whatever brain power we may have to learn and develop mental skills is a gift from God. In Christianity, you are open to learning all that you can about how this world works, because such knowledge is tracing how God organized the world. Being creative in how you handle what you learn becomes an expression of the image of the creator in you.

4. RESPONSIBILITY: Parents rejoice when their baby takes responsibility for putting food in her own mouth and for dressing herself. By doing so, the child is adding the dimension of being responsible for herself. A person at any stage of life who recognizes that, "If it's to be, it's up to me," is developing this dimension of the soul.

Many people find life distressing. Each case involves its own specific stress factors, but handling those factors depends in large measure upon the individual taking responsibility for his or her own reactions. A soul with a dimension of responsibility thinks, *What can I do about this?* It seeks solutions rather than seeking someone to blame.

The soul that expands into this fourth dimension will take responsibility for putting effort and discipline into learning, and will take responsibility for the choice of groups with whom to belong. Being a Christian means being responsible to God for how you use your brains, strength and opportunities to solve your own problems and be helpful to others.

However, it is possible to assume too much responsibility for aspects of life that you don't have the ability or opportunity to do anything constructive about. This can lead to unnecessary anxiety or guilt. Christianity leads you to be responsible for doing that which you are able while leaving in the hands of God that which you cannot do anything about. This surrender of such matters to God is part of the responsibility of a Christian.

5. VISION: The dimension of vision involves seeing not just what is visible, but what could be visible. Doing a job or taking part in any enterprise has an extra dimension when your soul has a vision of where your involvement could lead.

Think of gender relationships. Young people are sexually attracted to each other, but a relationship that has only sexual attraction has only one dimension. If the relationship expands into personal friendship, a second dimension of belonging with each other is added. Knowing more and more about each other adds a third dimension. Responsibility for the welfare of the other brings maturity into the relationship. Visualizing the possibility of spending a whole life together in marriage and parenthood adds yet another significant dimension. The demands children make on parents are easier to endure if one maintains a constant vision of the adults these children are going to be.

Your soul expands when you plan a project, work for a cause, or invest yourself in a venture you consider worthwhile. You are seeing the larger picture before it has become visible and the soul borrows initiative from the possibilities of the future. A project can enhance your way of earning a living. A goal brings you into relationships with new groups of people with whom you find belonging by sharing the same vision. Most visions require knowledge to pursue their potential.

However, vision is not necessarily good. Vision that is mostly negative about the possibilities of the future can depress the soul. Jesus said, *"Do not be anxious about tomorrow… Let the day's own trouble be sufficient for the day"* (Matthew 6:34). Christianity promotes trusting God for strength and guidance to handle whatever tomorrow brings.

It is possible to develop a vision that turns into a dangerous or destructive career. Hitler had a vision that propelled him into a position of power, but caused immense evil in Europe. Terrorists are a contemporary example of souls motivated by a destructive vision.

When your soul is tuned to God in Christ, your vision gets caught up in the larger vision of all humans living the purposes of God. Jesus called this "the kingdom of heaven." (In his day, a kingdom was where people did what the King wanted them to do.) Your faith manifests the power of the creator working through you, and helps you to choose goals that further God's purposes.

6. MORALITY: One's life always impinges on others. A moral dimension of the soul opens you to awareness of the effect your attitudes and actions have on others. It involves being careful to avoid activity that can damage them or the things they depend on.

Parents, communities or governments encourage morality with expectations or laws. God gave the Ten Commandments, and Jesus showed and taught living with love. God says, *"I will put my law within them, and I will write it upon their hearts"* (Jeremiah 31:33). Taking responsibility to make moral decisions, whether or not these decisions are set out by some authority, adds a moral dimension to your soul. God leads you to feel instinctively that a business deal is only good when it provides a good result for both parties involved and neither one takes advantage of the other.

Christian morals are grounded in Jesus' teaching and example. He taught, *what you would want others to do to you, do the same to them.* On one occasion, a young man asked Jesus what he should do to inherit eternal life. Jesus replied, *"Keep the commandments,"* and listed: *"You shall not kill, You shall not commit adultery, You shall not steal, You shall not bear false witness. Honour your father and your mother, and, you shall love your neighbour as yourself"* (Matthew 19:17–19).

A parent's responsibility for the best interests of their children will mean teaching them good morals by words and example and also limiting what they may do until they are experienced enough to handle responsibility for their own conduct.

Unfortunately, a moral dimension can get twisted into an attitude of being too judgmental of others and too harsh with those who fail. Christianity upholds high expectations, yet seeks to restore rather than punish those who don't meet those expectations.

7. LOVE: Love is a mystery that enriches relationships and affects everything you think or do. The love parents have for their children involves emotional attachment and nurture that prepares the young people to eventually leave the home. This parting may cause sadness, but love tempers this with joy that the young person can now function in a larger society.

This seventh dimension of love enriches all the other dimensions. It adds motivation for morality and flavour to your visions. Love develops a vision of sharing responsibility for community. Love expands the dimension of knowing by sensing how others experience life. Belonging relationships are enriched by blending concern for self with concern for others.

Love is wonderful, but it may turn to possessiveness with unrealistic expectations of the loved one and focus on the self. Then it is becoming first-dimensional. Christian love tempers possessiveness by seeing each person as one God loves, and cares about the way things feel for the other.

Love is basic to Christianity. In 1 Corinthians, we read,

> If I speak in the tongues of men and of angels and have not love, I am a noisy gong or a clanging cymbal… If I have understanding… knowledge… and faith, but have no love, I am nothing.
>
> Love is patient and kind; Love is not jealous or boastful, it is not arrogant or

rude; Love does not insist on its own way; It is not irritable or resentful. It does not rejoice at catching another in the wrong, but rejoices in the truth. Love bears all things, hopes all things, endures all things; Love never ends. As for prophecies, tongues and knowledge, they will pass away. So faith hope and love abide, these three, but the greatest of these is love. (1 Corinthians 13:1–13)

Christian love is expressed beautifully in the prayer attributed to Francis of Assisi:

Lord, make me an instrument your peace.
   Where there is hatred, let me sow love.
   Where there is injury, pardon.
   Where there is doubt, faith,
   Where there is despair, hope.
   Where there is darkness, light.
   Where there is sadness, joy.
O divine Master, Grant that I should not so much seek
   to be consoled, as to console;
   to be understood as to understand,
   to be loved as to love.

Love would seem to be the dimension least apt to turn negative, but the love of one's own people has been known to turn into indifference, or even hatred of others beyond their own circle. The purpose of love is distorted when one tries to enhance love by developing a joint hostility against another individual or group. The love of Jesus in one's soul leads to compassion for those one doesn't know personally, or even those one dislikes. Christians don't hate anyone.

THE SIGNIFICANCE OF THESE DIMENSIONS

Each dimension of the soul facilitates possibilities, but each soul chooses how it will handle the situation. The soul that focuses only on one or two of these dimensions and neglects the others lacks the fullness of life that could be possible in a balance of all dimensions. As you expand your soul in more dimensions, your own experience tells you that these dimensions are very real. You find each new dimension has potential for enriching your experience of life.

If you look at how all-encompassing these dimensions can be, you will notice that each dimension can become damaging to yourself or others, if you grab for a quick way to get results. Each dimension has a wholesome edge, and crossing that edge inadvertently or intentionally can lead you into bad territory.

In my youth, I lived on a farm at the edge of the Ottawa Valley where the agricultural land meets the rocky Precambrian Shield. We cultivated fields of agricultural soil, while beyond them the land became shallow with granite rock exposed or close to the surface. Rainwater could not cut channels in the rock to drain off, so this water collected in pools called swales or lay in flat marshes that grew bull rushes.

A variety of forest life grew there—sometimes isolated scraggly trees or tall timbers in groves, or cedar swamps so thick you had to push the branches aside to get through. There were also clear spaces where the rock was on the surface and nothing could grow. Here, footsteps left no prints behind for one to follow.

Once you crossed our back fence, you were in wild country that stretched ten miles wide from McNab Township Road to Highway 511 at Calabogie, and five miles deep to the uninhabited north shore of White Lake. This was fifty square miles of wild country.

As children, we were warned never to cross that back fence, or we could get lost. Only when we were older were we allowed to go out in that wild country to pick blueberries, hunt venison or look for lost cattle. There were reasons to be out there, but it was important to know what to do if you lost your way.

When I first ventured out there alone, my father explained to me that when people realize they are lost, their tendency is to panic and rush about, only to become more lost. He emphasized that I should be mentally aware that I could get lost, and thus should decide in advance what I would do if that happened.

His explicit instructions were, "As soon as you sense you are lost, bend your knees, sit on your heels and think. That posture keeps you from rushing about foolishly. You have lost the path. Accept that fact. Rather than thinking desperately about your immediate surroundings, lift your thoughts to the larger context.

"Draw upon all you know about the lay of the land, and think about what lies in each direction beyond this wild country. Clarify your mind about which direction our farm is from there.

"Don't stand up until you have established the direction of home and have formed a plan in your mind for moving in that direction. Then stand up and walk in the direction you have identified as leading toward home. You will still have to navigate the swales and swamps, get around the large rocks, and pass through the deep bush. This may not be as simple as following a beaten path, but always keep aware of the right direction while you figure out the way around each obstacle."

I will always remember Dad's conclusion: "Walking consistently in the right direction will bring you home. You will know you are safe, and can walk without fear." That advice has brought me home more times than I can count.

When you cross the wholesome edge in any dimension of the soul and find yourself thinking and acting in ways that can be destructive to yourself or to others, you are getting lost. Then Dad's advice is relevant: "As soon as you realize you are lost, bend your knees (figuratively if not physically)." Pray for renewal of your sense of God and the larger context of life. Think, *In what direction lies God's purpose?* When you get your sense of direction sorted out, make plans to move in that direction.

Then stand up (figuratively and physically). Stand tall above the urges of inner desires or the opinions of others and move in the direction of God's purpose.

Keep to that direction as you figure out how to navigate the immediate issues, and God will be with you as you move into being your best self again. Walk consistently in that direction and, "You will know you are safe and can walk without fear."

CHAPTER TWO

My Path to a Living Faith

I will share with you the path that my spiritual journey has taken. I don't mean to suggest that this is the only way, but I hope that it may help you think about your own path.

I grew up on a backwoods farm over a mile from our nearest neighbours. They had no children, so as a child, my own family unit was my world. It included four children, two parents and two older aunts, one a sister of my mother's mother and the other a sister of my father's mother. We were thus a three-generation family, although I never knew any of my grandparents. There would generally be a hired man living with us and often a school teacher boarding with us. This was our world. Television and computers had not yet been invented.

We went to church on Sundays as a family, but we didn't talk much about it. My parents thus exposed me

to the Christian Church and Christian attitudes to life,
but they made little mention of theories about God.

My mother had a strong faith and was actively involved in church, especially the Women's Missionary Society. My dad was strong on honesty and moral values.
He believed in making a contribution to his community
and country, doing what he could in areas of public service. He lived that philosophy and would be involved in
any activity he felt served the good of people.

Dad served in the Army during the first Great War,
and was active in the Canadian Legion, becoming
branch president, then Zone Commander. He served
on the council for the township and as reeve on County Council. He served as an elder in the church and as
Clerk of Session. He managed campaigns for members
of parliament, chaired the County School Board and the
board of a farmers' poultry-killing plant. He also helped
organize the county Federation of Agriculture and was
its first president.

When I was fourteen, my parents took me out of
school to work on the farm. This was common is those
days, but it isolated me from other young people. During workdays with Dad, I absorbed much of his philosophy of life. Dad taught me to speak in public and
think logically. I had very little social life during my teen
years, and compensated by reading books. Mother's
aunt had a collection of classic books and Dad brought
home books from the public library.

One summer, my mother persuaded me to go to a
teen camp sponsored by the Young People's Union,

which was a strong movement in the United Church at that time. I went to that camp, looking forward to having a good social time, living in tents with other young people, and it was good fun.

It also gave me something I had not expected. It introduced me to the mystery of God in nature and the spirit of Christ in the tone of our week together. I began to feel there was something significant about Christianity. The powerful closing service of the camp, which employed the symbolism of fire, was the first time I experienced the presence of God.

Back home on the farm, my new awareness of God faded. A few years later, my health gave me trouble. I had tonsillitis, but the doctor said he could not take my tonsils out until the inflammation went down. When it did, there was farm work pressing, and the operation was postponed. My energy level dropped. I felt sad, weary and discouraged.

At this point, I didn't know whether or not I believed in God, but I remembered the experience of camp. Through the Young People's Union, I sought out people like the camp leaders and they suggested I attend their weekly Bible study and prayer meetings. I found a warm fellowship that was very supportive, and praying with them regularly lifted my spirits.

The people I met there seemed to have an inner glow, which they defined as the effects of having been saved by Christ's crucifixion. When I inquired about this, they told me that God held all people guilty for the sin of Adam and this could not be forgiven unless a sinless man suffered for it. God had sent his son to die a horrible death to pay for sin, and this saved us from hell.

My whole sense of right and wrong rebelled against the idea of punishing an innocent party to avoid dealing with guilty ones. My knowledge from reading was enough to make me aware that holding descendants guilty for things done by their ancestors was the stuff of family feuds and ethnic prejudice. These can turn ugly if combined with a belief that forgiveness is not possible unless blood is shed.

I couldn't believe that the God whom Jesus called father, the creator of this amazing world, was so limited that he had to have his beloved son suffer through a crucifixion before he could forgive us. They said there was no other way he could avoid having to put all of us in hell. I was shocked! This wasn't the God I was coming to know in this fellowship. If I could (and should) forgive without requiring anyone to suffer, why couldn't God?

I talked with them about how I'd found the reality of God in their fellowship, but also how I couldn't believe this theory about God. At first they tried unsuccessfully to convince me. Then one member of the group said to me, "Give yourself to God unconditionally and devote yourself to living for God. Then you will discover what you can believe."

This was the most helpful thing anyone could have said to me about Christianity. In effect, I was told to live it instead of puzzling about intellectual theories. I made a decision to do what I felt God would want me to do and trust in him to see me through whatever life brought.

I surrendered my life to God, as revealed in Jesus' life and teaching. Jesus demonstrates love for people, so God would expect me to love the people I encountered and to act in ways that would be best for their well-being. I could not know with any certainty how to go about this, and I recognized that my efforts would inevitably be less than they ought to be. I decided to honestly try to live for God with dedication and learn more about how to do so as I went along. I didn't expect to be perfect, but trusted that God in his love would understand my limitations.

I began each day with prayer, committing the day to God. I tried to do each activity I got involved in as an offering to God. This affected the way I felt about tasks and relationships. I had no thought of earning favours from God. I just trusted God to be with me and give me strength and guidance for dealing with people and situations. I started reading the Bible and seeking nourishment of my relationship with God, rather than sorting out correct ideas to believe.

I was conscious that I had found this relationship with God through fellowship with people who had an obvious faith, and therefore realized that I needed fellowship with such people. I felt that God, who created the whole universe, could not be confined to any specific human institution. However, Christianity provided a place where I might find people who were reaching out to God, and the church I had grown up in was available.

The church services seemed different now that I was actively relating to God. I listened to sermons looking for insights and often heard things that applied directly to my situation. Praying with the minister in the midst of a praying congregation lifted my soul.

I found hymns such as:

> Breathe on me breath of God,
>> fill me with life anew,
> that I may love what thou dost love
>> and do what thou wouldst do.

and

> O Master, let me walk with thee,
>> in lowly paths of service free
> Teach me thy secret, help me bear
>> the strain of toil, the fret of care
> Teach me thy patience, still with thee,
>> in closer dear company,
> In work that keeps faith sure and strong,
>> in trust that triumphs over wrong.

These and other similar hymns touched on what I was seeking. They gave expression to my prayers. Singing with the congregation made me feel I was not alone, although I never learned to sing well.

The services and congregation were the same as they had been for years, but now it helped my soul to be part of it. I found myself lifted by being in tune with God.

Daily life did not change all that much, but I had changed. I put my humble efforts in the context of the power that created everything, and God's love transformed the way I felt about things and people. I never did get my tonsils out (I still have them). My energy came back and I could work with even better vigour than before. There were still discouragements, but God's love carried me.

I didn't have a sudden experience of being saved, but over a period of several months I found myself changing. Bible passages such as *"The fruit of the spirit is love, joy, peace, patience, kindness, goodness faithfulness, gentleness and self-control"* (Galatians 5:2) spoke of the reality that was coming alive within me.

The fruit metaphor was appropriate. One cannot manufacture a fruit. It appears by itself on a plant or tree that has been cultivated. I did not make love, joy, peace or patience happen. They just seemed to be part of a relationship of faith in God. All I can say is that I felt more whole.

I went to a young people's weekend conference and met a beautiful girl named Eunice. We began seeing one another regularly. Dad agreed to sell me the smaller of the two farms he was farming. Eunice and I were married and settled down to farm. Life was good.

Living with God brought me to care about people God loves, and made me feel that I should contribute to their well-being. I came to believe that a relationship with God could have this same effect in other people's lives, and that I should do what I could to help them find what I had found. How was I to go about this? Introducing God into a conversation seemed to make people feel like they were being put down or that I was trying to appear better than I was. Such reactions kept them from hearing me when I attempted to share my faith. How could I talk about it without stirring up defensiveness?

I taught Sunday school and talked about faith at young people's rallies. Ministers asked me to handle worship services for them. Leading a congregation in worship was a place where people wanted to hear about God. I learned that there was a severe shortage of ministers at that time and came to feel that God could be calling me into church ministry.

I looked into what would be required to become a minister and found that I would have to complete high school, then take six years of further education. That seemed impossible. I had a wife and two children to support. My wife did not have a paying job. My parents were strongly opposed to my leaving farming and going into the ministry, so I was financially on my own. I was buying my own farm, which I would have to give up.

Eunice and I talked and prayed about it for months. We attended a midsummer cemetery service and the minister talked about the shortness of life. He pictured a clock going *tick-tock, tick-tock*, each tick and tock marking one less second in my life. If there is something that God wants you to do, you had better be about it. At that moment, I knew the decision was made! I would do whatever it took to follow God's guidance. Eunice felt it, too. We ceased to talk about whether to do what ministry would require and began to organize termination of the farm business so that I could begin to study in September.

I finished five years' worth of high school in ten months, living on capital we obtained by closing out the farm business. Then we managed to survive economically through my serving rural congregations while I got involved in formal university education.

LOGIC IN THEOLOGY

Eager to know all I could, I found that a degree in arts provided a great privilege to read and learn. When I got to theological college, it troubled me that Christian doctrines were arbitrarily declared to be truth, with little logical basis. The professors seemed to be rationalizing positions taken by past theologians. I was concerned about the honesty of accepting ideas as truth that had an inadequate logical basis.

I talked about this with a professor, Dr. Donald Mathers, who recommended that I write my degree thesis on that topic. I researched everything I could find that had been written on the philosophy of knowledge and theology and wrote a thesis called *The Logic of Theological Language.*[1]

I came to the insight that serious reasoning develops out of one or more basic presuppositions that are seldom recognized. They are simply and often unconsciously believed. They are thus articles of faith. These presuppositions give rise to questions. Thinking people in a culture develop hypotheses to answer these questions. These are educated guesses which can be tested

---

1   The thesis is available in the library of Queen's Theological College.

by empirical investigation. If the evidence verifies them, they are now based on empirical investigation and qualify as knowledge.

It is important to note that absolute presuppositions and conclusions are not the same. The presupposition comes first, as a faith position that is simply believed without proof. When people formulate answers to the questions raised by the presupposition, these answers are conclusions.

The basic absolute presupposition cannot be proved or disproved. Answers to the questions it raises should be subjected to rigorous investigation before they become accepted as part of the knowledge base that is the foundation for civilizations.

An example we all live with is the basic presupposition that cause-and-effect relationships found to be true here and now will be true in all places and at all times. This is an absolute presupposition that cannot be proved or disproved because we cannot test it in all places at all times. This presupposition seems natural to people raised in a civilization that functions on knowledge that is based on it.

It takes an effort of mind to recognize that this basic presupposition was not always believed. Study of the history of knowledge shows that cultures which did not believe in the universality and reliability of cause-and-effect relationships did not develop science. Believing this presupposition without proof was a necessary precondition for development of the knowledge which has enabled humans to develop a lifestyle that is amazingly better than at any other period in human history.

Many people tend to think that knowledge is based on observation and that faith is an addition of things we cannot observe. Actually, the knowledge we gain from observation is quite primitive compared to the sophisticated knowledge that begins as faith in an absolute presupposition. Hypothetical answers to the resulting questions are "educated guesses" which instigate empirical investigation and result in knowledge that is based on observation. Most people are unaware of this process that began with faith.

The whole body of scientific knowledge we trust and live with rests upon a few absolute presuppositions that are believed, but are not subject to proof. Believing the basic presuppositions without proof is logical. It is an act of faith that is essential to the whole knowledge process. Believing the answers without proof is not logical, since they are conclusions and subject to verification.

This is further complicated by the fact that verified conclusions often fill the role of further presuppositions that raise more questions that become part of the process that expands available knowledge. Such secondary presuppositions are thus vital to the growth of knowledge, but they are still conclusions and still subject to further investigation and rejection or verification.

Understanding this concept enabled me to recognize that there is logical validity in believing that everything has been created by One who identifies with humans, and holds all humans responsible for treating each person as having eternal worth. This is an absolute presupposition that cannot be proved or disproved. It must be accepted on faith.

Christianity rests on this basic presupposition. However, this presupposition has raised questions that have stimulated people to seek answers. People throughout history have worked out answers to these questions in the light of their experience and the level of knowledge available to them.

In the process they have come to conclusions about God and human life. These conclusions are theories, not basic presuppositions. Therefore, they do not have the same claim to be accepted on faith as the absolute presupposition of God.

This distinction between the absolute presupposition and the relative conclusions is vital to understanding why Christianity believes in God without question, yet has at various points rethought its answers to the questions that faith in God raises.

Understanding this enabled me to think about theology. While accepting the basic absolute presupposition of God as crucial for faith, insisting that human conclusions in the form of theories must not be examined attributes divine authority to human constructions. This is the very nature of idolatry.

If all this seems complicated to grasp, here is the essence: people apparently need an intellectual framework to enable them to think and communicate about the mystery of God. The theories they have developed to give shape to their concept of God are human conclusions attempting to express the mystery of God for people in a specific time and place. They may be helpful in that context, but they need to be rethought from time to time to be sure that they express the mystery of God for people living in a different time.

Proper procedure in formal meetings allows a motion to be amended in many ways, but any amendment that negates the original motion is out of order and unacceptable. Adjustments to theories about God can be appropriate, but not if they negate the reality of God.

CHAPTER THREE

The Bible, What It Is

The Bible has been a significant factor in Christianity. So our consideration of Christianity should think about the Bible and questions like, what is the Bible and where did it come from?

The Bible is a book all Christians use to help them relate to God. The first thing that becomes apparent when we examine the contents of the Bible more closely is that it is not just one book, but many books. Examining those books, we can recognize that they were not all composed at the same time.

Writers use words and concepts derived from the world around them. For communication to happen, our words must bring to mind concepts that both the writer and the reader find familiar. People living in one time period would not be familiar with things common in a different time period. Understanding what is said and how it is said often reveals the time period when it was written.

For example, suppose you were to read an article that mentioned writing the original script with a typewriter. Then you read another article that mentions typing the original on a word processor into a computer. Would you think that both these articles were composed in the same time period? If an article uses the term 9/11 even casually, would you not recognize immediately that this material was composed in the year 2001 or later?

Paying close attention to the way things are said or what events are even casually mentioned in a book of the Bible yields an indication of the approximate time period during which that book was written. Knowledge of human history tells us that those time periods were spread over a very long time, and different books may sometimes be quite far apart. These writings have been preserved because they tell how those people in differing situations thought about the great mystery of God.

Parts of the Old Testament attribute to God some cruel attitudes and actions, like slaughtering the inhabitants of a country the people felt God had given them; this contrasts with the picture of God Jesus later reveals. It does not indicate a change in God, but a change in the thinking of the people, and is evidence that God did not write the Bible.

Jesus upheld the many passages which tell of God's caring. I value the Bible for this and because it is our link with the teaching and spirit of Jesus, and the working of his spirit in the Christian movement.

The Bible contains poetry, history, storytelling, prophetic inspiration, wisdom and apocalyptic writings. These are all to be appreciated for what they are, without making the mistake of assuming that everything in the Bible is history, poetry, or any other single type of literature.

Where did the Bible come from? Think of a map of the world. You will see that the great landmasses of Europe and Asia were joined to Africa at one point, where the Suez Canal is today. People living in the area east of that point of the planet in the distant past told stories aloud. Those stories used narrative form to deal with God's creation of the world, and God's interaction with specific people. They tell that God made a covenant with Noah and again with Abraham. God's care for their descendants brought them out of slavery in Egypt and gave them the Ten Commandments.

This was long before written language was invented, and each generation heard these stories from the preceding generation. We have no firm knowledge as to how much of each story was based on what really happened and how much was intuitive imagination to illustrate profound insights. The stories are valuable for those insights.

Approximately a thousand years before Christ, stories that had long been in the folklore of the people were written down, using the new technology of writing. They became the books of Genesis and Exodus in the Bible we know.

The next three books, containing a great many rules for living and for worship, were written in Hebrew years later. When these three were added to the first two, the five were preserved by the community on leather scrolls and known as the Law (the Torah, in Hebrew).

Several other books were written during the next centuries. They also include both history and imaginative stories to illustrate their convictions. The great prophets of 800 to 600 B.C.E. were inspired to write or have others write their messages from God. More books were written later. The Psalms were the hymns of the people of God.

Around 300 B.C.E., these Hebrew writings were translated into Greek, which had become the language of the Mediterranean world. More books written in Greek were added. This collection of literature, which was composed over a thousand years, was the Bible that Jesus knew.

After Jesus' death and resurrection, the first Christian churches collected Paul's letters, the gospel writings, and other literature of the Christian movement. They decided these were a New Testament of Holy Scripture and called the older scripture the Old Testament.

The Catholic Church translated both testaments into Latin and called this the Vulgate. They taught that the Vulgate was the very words of God, but could only be understood if interpreted by the Catholic Church. The Jews held a council at which they rejected the Old Testament books written in Greek and designated only those books written originally in Hebrew to be the authentic Holy Scripture.

People attempting to reform the Roman Catholic Church claimed the Holy Scriptures or Bible as their authority. To avoid the Roman Catholic Church's interpretation of the Bible, they translated the original Greek New Testament and the Hebrew Old Testament into the languages of Europe. They considered this the authentic Holy Scriptures, and it forms the background of the Bible that is now used by Protestant Christians in many languages. The Old Testament books originally written in Greek were left out, but they are sometimes printed in the back of Bibles as the Apocrypha.

Today there are many versions of the Bible available. Some are authorized versions such as the King James, the Revised Standard Version, the New English version and the Jerusalem Bible. Authorized means that they were translated by teams of scholars from several denominations to ensure accuracy to the original languages without bias.

Other versions are available, such as the Living Bible and the Good News Bible. These versions paraphrase passages to make them easier to read, but their paraphrases are often influenced by the particular theology of one stream of Christianity.

I believe we should recognize in the Bible the message of God's love, as it is revealed in the spirit of Jesus and can be seen in the law and the prophets. Used selectively, these passages can inspire, because they provide memorable words to express a mystery that is real.

THINKING ABOUT GOD IN THE BIBLE

In the book of Exodus, we read that a man named Moses had an encounter with God. It happened on a mountain, but the narrative leading up to the occasion reveals that Moses had been touched early in life by the love of a mother who risked her baby in a basket on a river to protect him. Moses then experienced the compassion of a king's daughter who cared about this baby and brought him up in her home.

The love of these two women nurtured a mystery of compassion in Moses that stirred him to anger when he saw a Hebrew slave being beaten. He reacted impulsively and killed the Egyptian doing the beating. This put Moses in danger, so he fled to the wilderness and established a new life as a shepherd.

One day on a mountain alone with the sheep, he witnessed a fire that did not burn all its fuel and go out. If we get sidetracked by the physical issue of why the fire did not burn itself out, we can miss the point. Think deeper and ask yourself about that fire which time would not burn out. Was that fire the burning compassion within Moses about the condition of the Hebrews?

Moses became conscious of a powerful and mysterious presence that spoke out of that fire. There was no other human around, yet he realized he was not alone! With him was a Presence identified as the God of his ancient ancestor Abraham, whose memory lingered in the culture of the Hebrews. God told Moses that he also was concerned about the Hebrews and would free them from slavery. God would do this through Moses.

Moses learned two important points in this encounter:

1. God cares about powerless people being oppressed.
2. God acts by sending someone to do something about it.

Moses protested, "Who am I that I should do this?"

Good question. Let us think about how this question could be answered, breaking it into relevant parts:

1. Who could be accepted as a leader by the Hebrews? Answer: One who was of the Hebrew race.
2. What member of the Hebrew race could talk to the King? Kings were not easy to approach, especially not by slaves. Answer: One who had been raised in a king's household.
3. Who could guide a crowd of free slaves in the wilderness? Answer: One who had shepherded sheep in the area for years.
4. Who could govern a crowd of freed slaves? Answer: One who had spent his growing years observing the government in Egypt.

Reading the Bible with awareness tells us that Moses was probably the only person who filled all these requirements. Have you noticed that God often prepares a person for a task without their awareness?

Is this story true? We have no way of verifying it as factual, but it is well known that many individuals have been disturbed by seeing people suffer from various causes, and this compassion burned within them. Out of that fire they were conscious of God saying, "I care about these people, too, and I want you to do what you can about it."

You may have heard about, or known personally, people for whom this has been a turning point, leading them to change their direction and try to make a difference for people. Often it involves facing much difficulty with only the assurance that God will be with them. Their lives have been changed, and so have the lives of those they have helped. The mystery that inspired them is invisible, but the results can be observed. There is profound truth in the story of the calling of Moses, whether or not it is historical.

Moses needed to tell the Hebrews about God, so he asked for God's name. God replied, *"I am who I am"* (Exodus 3:14), indicating that the mystery of God is the same sort of mystery we refer to when we say or think "I".

The Genesis account tells of Moses and the Hebrews moving out into the wilderness. They traveled toward a pillar of cloud by day and a pillar of fire at night. This is exactly what an erupting volcano looks like from a distance. It provided something impressive they could see as God going before them. They used an awe-inspiring factor in their circumstances as a means to relate to the mystery of God.

When they arrived at the volcanic mountain, the phenomenon of smoke and fire was localized, so they camped there. Moses went up on the mountain to consult with God. When he returned, he found that the people had made a golden calf to provide something more concrete they could worship.

This caused tension between those Hebrews who desired a god that was visible in a concrete way and those who believed in God who was mysterious and invisible. The dispute was resolved and the golden calf disposed of, but the desire for concrete physical or social structures upon which to base faith is still with us. The faith that became Christianity lives in those willing to follow and obey a mysterious God who is not limited to what can be seen, measured or localized.

THE TEN COMMANDMENTS

Moses came down from the mountain bringing written words from God in the form of the Ten Commandments (Exodus 20:1–17). These commands were for freshly freed slaves beginning a life of freedom, but they also define the way God created humans to live. These commandments are integral to Christianity and the last six have become part of the values in many civilizations that have been touched by Christianity.

Let us pause and notice that the concept of God was expanded at this point. The Hebrews had thought of God as supporting them, freeing them from slavery, saving them from the sea, etc. In these commandments, they were discovering that God also has very definite requirements he expects his people to follow. Both these views of God were carried into Christianity.

These commandments are basic and cannot be changed, but how these commandments are to be applied in specific circumstances has to be thought through. Let us think about each one.

1. "I am the Lord your God… You shall have no other gods before me."

This is basic. Do not treat any of the other mysteries in life that have a claim on you as God. The commandment does not say that you need to eliminate them, as they give life its wholeness, but do not let any one of them become what you live for.

2. "You shall not make for yourself… any likeness of anything… you shall not bow down to them or serve them."

Human ingenuity will develop church organizations and buildings, specific doctrines, or documents like scripture that help us sense the presence of God. These can be valuable for nurturing our relationship with God, and the commandment does not require us to eliminate them.

It says that we must not treat as God any of these things that were made by humans. Only God is God.

3. "You shall not take the name of the Lord your God in vain."

Any word or action you do or say before God is sacred. You must be completely serious about it and follow through on all it implies.

4. "Remember the sabbath day, to keep it holy."

Things get done if we schedule them. Fit into your schedule one day a week to rest and renew body and soul in God's presence. You must also give that day of rest to those who work for you.

5. "Honor your father and your mother."

Respect those who gave you life and cared for you before you could look after yourself. Thereby you are respecting the sacredness of having been given life. This includes respect for the structures of your society that were here for you when you began and within which you shape your life.

6. "You shall not kill."

Treat every human life as sacred. Do not destroy any human life physically, nor destroy its capacity to become all it was created to be.

7. "You shall not commit adultery."

Humans do not arrive on the scene as mature adults. Each person begins as a helpless infant that needs many years of care to develop in body and soul. The quality of that care depends on a stable marriage. The commandment does not condemn sex, but is definite that you shall respect the sacredness of marriage—God's method of caring for kids—and never interfere with the sexual loyalty at the heart of marriage.

8. "You shall not steal."

The sacredness of each person's life includes their right to have property that they can own and use without interference. You must never take it from them by force, fraud or by denying them equal value.

9. "You shall not bear false witness."

The capacity to communicate with other human souls is key to all relationships. Truth in every communication is sacred. You must not tell lies about anything, especially lies that may get someone into trouble, nor deceive people for your own gain.

10. "You shall not covet your neighbour's house… wife… or anything that is your neighbour's."

Do not entertain thoughts that might lead you to break any of the commandments. Be content with life as you are able to make it work and do not envy what others have.

Each of these commands is negative: "You shall not."

The actions listed speak of things the soul might consider to be quick solutions to specific situations. God says "NO" when those quick fixes damage other people or significant values they depend on. Each commandment is not only to be obeyed, but defines who we are in a sacred relationship with our creator.

The Hebrews made a box to store the stone tablets with the commandments written on them. It was called the Ark of the Covenant. This box met their need for something concrete they could see, and preserved the word of God.

Notice the beginnings of scripture. Seeing God in the pillars of fire and cloud had inspired the Hebrews to escape the danger of being recaptured, and to face the unknown dangers of the wilderness. However, they had been limiting God to these phenomena, and that concept of God was too geographically limited to lead them any farther.

They needed a sense of God with them as they traveled, so they constructed a large tent that had a central room with exactly equal length, width and height. This was God's place and was called the Holy of Holies. It was empty, to symbolize that the presence of God could not be portrayed by any material thing. They called this tent a tabernacle. It was built of poles and curtains which they could dismantle and carry with them, to be set up again when they next made camp.

Pillars of cloud and fire had served these people in special circumstances, but they were not divine in themselves. The Hebrews had to abandon faith in cloud and fire so they could move on, taking with them a holy place and God's word in things they could see and touch.

Over time, the holy place has changed and the scriptures have developed, but God has not changed. Christians today are still helped in relating to God by a holy place and a bible. These, like the pillars of cloud and fire, are not divine in themselves.

The curtains around the holy space in the tabernacle marked out a place where people could focus on the mystery of God, but they did not confine God. Churches have doctrines about God that are like those curtains. They are made of words, ideas or theories to focus awareness on the mystery of God, but God is not confined by them.

The Hebrews wandered for years, barely surviving in a dry, barren desert, and finally settled in the land they believed God had promised them. Here the soil could produce food, but they had no experience with growing crops. They had to learn how to farm from those already farming. The local people believed that gods called Baals made the crops grow and the animals produce offspring. This Baal religion seemed integral to growing food, so there was much tension between loyalty to God and the economic needs that seemed to require worship of Baals.

The contemporary businessperson can get caught in the same situation as the Israelite farmers. Pressure to make the company's success the most important thing in life is significant, and its results can be measurable.

Responsibility to God for the spiritual needs of family, community and the powerless is invisible. It is a mystery in which the results cannot be quickly measured, but they are significant. The tension between whether to worship God or the contemporary equivalent of the Baals is still with us.

THE TEMPLE AND THE PROPHETS

The Israelites now had resources to build permanent residences. The king also built a house for God. This was an impressive structure made of stone and was called a temple. It maintained the empty, cube-shaped room to symbolize the invisible presence of God.

The focus of faith that had been designed to go with the people wherever they went was now replaced by a temple permanently set in one place. The curtains that had rustled with the breezes were replaced by rigid stone walls around the holy of holies. Rituals with appropriate sacrifices grew to be considered an important part of relating to God.

This tended to get many people again thinking of God as limited to one location, similar to the former thinking of God as located on the volcanic mountain.

This tendency to erect impressive buildings as a focus for faith has continued into Christianity. It can be observed in magnificent cathedrals and thousands of churches. These buildings are valuable for their symbolism, which can make us aware of God. Despite their significance, the buildings, rituals and doctrines are not divine. The mystery of God is the divine reality, and it can be known in other places by other means.

Awareness of this mystery is indicated in a statement found in Deuteronomy 6:4–6: *"Hear O Israel, the Lord our God is one Lord; and you shall love the Lord your God with all your heart, and with all your soul, and with all your might."* Love is mystery that cannot be seen, measured or localized. The significance the Israelites placed on this exhortation is indicated by their use of it as a sort of creed. We will also find that the religious leaders who criticized Jesus on other topics agreed with him immediately about this.

God's expectation that his people would do what would be good for others was expressed in the commandments. The Hebrew community expanded the commandments into a number of regulations to cover practical issues that might arise. To elicit respect for these, they attributed them to Moses. They can be found in the biblical books of Exodus, Leviticus, Numbers, and Deuteronomy.

Some of those laws may seem harsh when we have become accustomed to modern Christian values, but they were efforts to give practical shape to the divine command that God's people protect those with no one to defend them. They were formulated to enforce the will of God within the limitations of a people who had no police and no jails.

Leviticus 19:9–10 says, *"When you reap the harvest of your land, you shall not reap your field to its very border... you shall not strip your vineyard bare, neither shall you gather the fallen grapes of your vineyard; you shall leave them for the poor and the sojourner."*

This concern for the poor was kept alive by prophets who declared that focusing on sacrifices in the temple while ignoring the needs of the poor was not acceptable to God.

The prophet Amos declared that God says, *"I despise your feasts, and I take no delight in your solemn assemblies… but let justice roll down like waters, and righteousness like an ever-flowing stream"* (Amos 5:21, 24).

The prophet Micah put it this way: *"What does the Lord require of you, but to do justice, and to love kindness and to walk humbly with your God"* (Micah 6:8).

The prophet Isaiah writes, *"Is not this the fast that I choose: to loose the bonds of wickedness… to let the oppressed go free… to share your bread with the hungry and bring the homeless poor into your house… then shall your light break forth as the dawn"* (Isaiah 58:6–8). *"If you are willing and obedient, you shall eat the good of the land"* (Isaiah 1:19).

The mystery of God expressed through the message of the great prophets still inspires Christian people to care about those in need, and to express that care through actions designed to help.

The prophets also warned that God would punish the people with disasters if they did not live this compassion. *"Remove the evil of your doings from before my eyes; cease to do evil, learn to do good; seek justice, correct oppression, defend the fatherless, plead for the widow… if you are willing and obedient, you shall eat the good of the land; But if you refuse and rebel, you shall be devoured by the sword"* (Isaiah 1:16–20).

Again: *"The Lord enters into judgment with the elders and princes of his people: 'It is you who have devoured the vineyard, the spoil of the poor is in your houses'"* (Isaiah 3:14). And, *"What will you do on the day of punishment, in the storm which is to come from afar? Nothing remains but to crouch among the prisoners or fall among the slain"* (Isaiah 10:3–4).

There were two sides to the message proclaimed by the writing prophets:

1. God expected his people to care for the powerless.
2. Things could get very bad if they continued ignoring God's wishes.

These two emphases can be seen in the way Christianity developed. The spirit of Jesus embraced the prophetic compassion for the powerless, but the early Christian movement also emphasized the prophetic concept of a God that punished. Both had effects on the nature of theories that developed in Christianity.

THE EXILE IN BABYLON

At that time in history, powerful nations sent armies to conquer smaller nations and establish great empires. The Israelite nation was conquered by an empire that sought to establish control by selecting those among the occupied people who had leadership potential and moving them to the distant city of Babylon. This was designed on the theory that without leaders the conquered people would not resist the occupation.

In Babylon, the exiles were too far away to get to the temple for worship. Their belief that the mystery of God was located in the temple had to be rethought. A prophet named Ezekiel told the exiles of seeing God on a throne with wheels under it. He was using the new technology of wheels to illustrate that God's throne was mobile and not stationary at the temple. This enabled the exiles to picture that God was with them, even in a distant land.

Fixation on the temple as the only place to worship God still affects some Christians who believe God can only be known in their church. Ezekiel's vision still applies. God is not confined to any human structure or institution.

The exiles dealt with being unable to get to their holy building by emphasizing a holy time—the Sabbath day. They gathered in small groups each Sabbath to read the scriptures and pray together. These gatherings were the beginning of what became synagogues, an institution that enabled their faith to survive their tumultuous history.

Christianity began in similar gatherings they called churches. Whatever forms have been adopted since by various denominations, the regular weekly gatherings have continued to be the place where Christians renew their relationship with the mystery of God.

The exiles from Judah were called Jews. Being selected for exile because of their leadership potential meant their regular weekly meetings brought together people with intellectual potential to talk about their situation (note the resemblance to a university).

They had believed that God would protect their nation, but now they felt that God had allowed a foreign power to conquer them. They took seriously the warnings that God would punish them for not obeying his commandments and concluded that their present misfortune was God's punishment. They sought to avoid disobeying God again.

The exiles had brought their scriptures with them and believed God spoke to them through scripture. They applied their combined intellectual abilities to consider the implications of every word in the Torah and established what they thought was exactly how each admonition in scripture should be obeyed. This began a way of thinking about God that motivated the Pharisees in the New Testament and has carried over into some modern types of Christianity.

Another prophet, called Second Isaiah, told the exiles that their God is God of all the world, with a power that would bring them back to their homeland. *"Comfort, comfort my people, says your God... Behold, the Lord comes with might... He will lead his flock like a shepherd, he will gather the lambs in his arms, and he will carry them in his bosom and gently lead those that are with young. Fear not, I am with you... I will strengthen you, I will help you, I will uphold you with my victorious right hand"* (Isaiah 40:1,10–11 and Isaiah 41:10). Second Isaiah's words of hope were needed in the situation and have helped Christians in many difficult circumstances.

The exile of a few hundred Jews was a time of significant development in Judaism and the effects continued into Christianity. They are as follows:

1. God is God of all the world.
2. God will comfort and strengthen.
3. Scripture is a way to hear God's word.
4. Weekly gatherings became synagogues and then churches.

CHAPTER FOUR

The Influence of Other Cultures

PERSIAN

When Babylon was defeated by Persia, the King of Persia allowed the Jews to go back to Jerusalem, but the Israelite nation was now ruled by Persia. Few people are aware of the long-standing effect on Jewish religion that occurred during this Persian period, and which carried into Christianity.

Persian religion was known as Zoroastrian, and was based on belief in a god of light and a life beyond this physical life, where there would be reward and punishment. The righteous would go at death to a place of light and have pleasant experiences with Ahura Mazda, god of light. Those who had done evil would go to a place of darkness and be mistreated by Agra Mainu, god of darkness. These two gods, one that urges goodness and the other evil, were believed to be in conflict for the souls of humans.

Zoroastrian taught that evil deeds left a weight in the soul. After death, the soul had to cross a very narrow bridge to get to the place of light, but would fall off that bridge and drop into the darkness of hell if weighted with too much sin.

Hope had always been an element in the religion of Israel. The Hebrew slaves survived the wilderness through hope of a promised land. Prophets taught them to hope for a day of the Lord when God would bring justice and righteousness. Later, the exiles hoped for a day when they would return to their land and God's kingdom would be realized there.

When the return to Jerusalem brought continued occupation under the apparently invincible power of Persia, this hope for a better life faded. The Persian faith offered a vision of a good life beyond death, with the enemy getting punished. The Persian god of light demanded an ethic that was similar to the great prophets and could be identified with the Jewish God. Many Jews took these Persian ideas into their faith, and the concepts of heaven, and hell with a devil and many evil spirits became part of Jewish faith that continued into Christianity.

GREEK AND ROMAN

The Jewish people continued to deal with occupation by a series of empires. After Babylon and Persia, Alexander the Great established a Greek empire and insisted on the Greek language being used, making it the universal language of the area. The Jews translated their Hebrew scriptures into Greek, and early Christian literature was written in Greek. This contributed to the spread of Christianity, because literate people in Mediterranean countries could read Greek and were thus able to read the scriptures.

The Greek Empire split into two parts, one in Egypt and one in Mesopotamia. These two Greek empires fought with each other from time to time. Israel was geographically located between them, so when great armies from one side would attack the other, they came across Israel. In those days, armies did not carry their own provisions, but seized food supplies from people along the way and killed anyone who resisted. To escape this situation, many Jews fled their homeland and formed communities of Jews in surrounding countries.

The Roman Empire defeated the Greeks and stopped these wars, but the Israelite lands were still under foreign domination by Rome. Many Jews hoped God would arrange for a descendant of David to be king of Israel. He would end foreign occupation, bringing peace and righteousness. Kings in that culture were anointed, not crowned, so the expected king was called the Messiah (the Anointed One).

APOCALYPTIC

A new style of scripture appeared around this time, called Apocalyptic. This predicted a future time when God would intervene and deliver the people from evil. The message in Apocalyptic writing was that things may be bad and they will get worse, but God will be with you, enabling you to endure the terrible times. Then God will bring you into a new and brighter day. Some felt that this could only happen if this world were first destroyed, and developed an expectation of an end to this world.

This writing has been called prophecy in order to give it an authority associated with the great writing prophets, but it is not prophetic. The great writing prophets have a timeless message about justice and righteousness that speaks to every age. Apocalyptic writing has a different purpose. It is literature written in times of great trouble to encourage hope that, no matter how bad things get, God is going to triumph in the end and so will his people.

When Jesus' followers experienced persecution, apocalyptic writing also appeared in parts of the Bible, especially in the book of Revelation, which states, *"Here is a call for the endurance of the saints, those who keep... the faith of Jesus."* (Revelation 14:12). This book presents a vision of terrible things to be expected, but concludes with God triumphing over evil. *"God himself will be with them; he will wipe away every tear from their eyes, and death shall be no more, neither shall there be mourning nor crying nor pain any more… He who sat on the throne said, 'Behold I make all things new'"* (Revelation 21:3–5).

Some Christians have interpreted apocalyptic literature as foretelling history which includes an imminent end of the world, and have even figured out dates for these things to happen. So far, these dates have passed without incident.

I believe that the message in this literature is encouragement. Our situations may seem terrible at times and could become worse, but God will see us through. God will triumph and bring his people into a better place. This message is an integral part of Christianity that gets confused if people try to deduce specific dates or events. I do not believe that apocalyptic writings foretell exact events that can be expected to occur.

CHAPTER FIVE

Jesus of Nazareth

Jesus was born into a Jewish culture that had been shaped by all these historical factors. Its faith was based in the faith of Moses and the prophets, localized by the temple and the nation, and crystallized by the legalism of the exile. It was overlaid with Persian ideas of heaven, hell, a devil, and a host of evil spirits. It was infused with ideas of a coming Messiah who would fix everything and ideas of the imminent end of the world. It was also simmering with resentment at foreign occupation.

This was the milieu in which Jesus lived and taught. It would have its effect on the methods he used to communicate with those practicing Judaism in that time. Typical is his teaching about evil spirits. Jesus was demonstrating the power of God over evil. In a culture where most of his listeners believed evil spirits caused illness, Jesus used this concept as one they could appreciate.

Some Jews who were called Pharisees believed that the words in the scripture were the exact words of God and that the system of obeying these, which had been developed during the exile, should be enforced in the nation. This way of thinking can still be found in churches that believe the words of the Bible are the literal words of God.

Other Jews called Sadducees believed that worship centred in the temple was the only way to God. This way of thinking can be seen in Christians who believe that the only way to relate to God is through their church.

These ways of thinking have had value in providing people with a setting for relating to the mystery of God. Treating them as the only way to God, however, is giving divine status to human constructs. In logical terms, it is treating conclusions as though they were absolute presuppositions. The danger in absolutism can be seen in the way both Pharisees and Sadducees resented Jesus and eventually plotted together to have him killed.

A man named John held revival gatherings at which he called upon the people to change their way of thinking as well as their actions. Those of his hearers who wanted to turn their lives to doing what God expected were baptized by John in the Jordan River to symbolize beginning a new life. Jesus came from Nazareth to hear John and was baptized by him.

That baptism was such an experience of the spirit of God that Jesus went off by himself in the wilderness to meditate on what it meant. When he returned, he began his public ministry. Matthew tells us, *"From that time,*

Jesus began to preach, saying, 'repent for the kingdom of heaven is at hand'" (Matthew 4:17).

Jesus revealed God as a loving God. He demonstrated this through his own attitudes and the stories he told. He knew the scriptures and affirmed passages which revealed God's compassion and God's expectation that his people would care for the powerless. Jesus taught that actions expressing this love were closer to the will of God than exact obedience to scripture. He was calling people back to the mystery at the core of their ancient religion.

Belief in God's love still lingered in the souls of most Jews, so Jesus' message was welcomed by the crowds who came to hear him. He attracted many followers and chose twelve of them to learn from him and called them his disciples.

In living the love he taught, Jesus associated with people that religious leaders felt holy men should avoid. Jesus taught an ethic of love that often did not insist on exact obedience to the law and was opposed by the Pharisees.

Jesus befriended Zacchaeus and took Matthew, who worked for a foreign power, into his group of disciples. This did not uphold the popular conviction that God cared only for the Jewish people. The Pharisees and the Sadducees had their disagreements with each other, but they agreed that Jesus' popularity could change the religion of the people. They decided his influence should be stopped.

They arranged to have Jesus executed by the Roman governor. Roman soldiers carried out this execution in their customary form, by nailing Jesus to a cross and leaving him to hang there and die. Loyal followers took his body and placed it in a tomb.

The people who knew Jesus had found in this man closeness to God and an inner wholeness that was healing to illness, affirming to the worth of individuals, accepting and restoring for sinners, and caring for the weak and powerless.

When John the Baptist sent messengers to ask of Jesus, "Who are you?" Jesus told them to look at what was happening around him: *"The blind receive their sight and the lame walk, lepers are cleansed and the deaf hear, and the dead are raised up, and the poor have good news"* (Matthew 11:5). Jesus came into his home synagogue and read from Isaiah, *"The Spirit of the Lord is upon me, because he has anointed me to preach good news to the poor. He has sent me to proclaim release to the captives, to set at liberty those that are oppressed"* (Luke 4:18).

What had been happening around Jesus was bigger than could be neatly wrapped up in words. Life for these people was not easy. There was much suffering, oppression and cruelty. With Jesus, there was a vision of God's kingdom where people loved and cared for each other, and where justice and righteousness prevailed. He inspired an unbounded hope!

Then disaster struck! The man of love and peace was killed with a cruelty designed to terrify any who might be following him. They were struck with something more than sorrow. The whole dynamic that surrounded Jesus had collapsed. They experienced the end of a great vision. Having known such heights made the crash even more devastating.

THEN HE CAME BACK!

People told about Jesus' return in differing ways. The women found the tomb empty. Two on the road to Emaus walked with Jesus, but did not know it until he broke bread with them. The discouraged disciples were in a locked room and suddenly Jesus stood among them. The disciples on a lakeshore dejectedly returned to their former work of fishing, and Jesus walked to them on the water. They shared fish with him on the shore, and Jesus told Peter, *"Feed my sheep"* (John 21:17).

The disciples were gathered together in Jerusalem, and suddenly Jesus stood among them and said, *"It is I myself; handle me, and see; for a spirit has not flesh and bones as you see that I have"* (Luke 24:39).

These stories don't fit into each other. In some, Jesus appears and disappears suddenly; in others he eats fish and encourages Thomas and others to touch him. The physical details of these events are not the point. They were told many years after the event. The reality was in Jesus' living spirit with his followers. With Jesus, the whole vision was still possible! The dynamic that surrounded Jesus could live again, because Jesus lived again.

This man so filled with God had not been defeated! They were convinced that he could never be defeated. God was in Christ and could be felt by those who walked with him. They called this the Holy Spirit and it manifested new life within them. The New Testament expresses this in many ways, such as, *"If any one is in Christ, he is a new creation"* (2 Corinthians 5:17), and *"We have been born anew to a living hope through the resurrection of Jesus"* (1 Peter 1:3).

Resurrection does not provide a formula for getting into heaven so much as it renews awareness that God can be very near and personal in Jesus, and that the whole purpose in human life demonstrated by Jesus cannot be defeated.

The evil that killed Jesus is real. Today we can feel the reality of evil in the news about destructive events and troubles in many places, even in our own countries or communities. We can easily feel that the world is a terrible place, and become cynical. The despair that hit the disciples after Jesus' crucifixion can affect us and hinder our capacity to deal with life.

The resurrection is a mystery that changed Jesus' little group of followers and can change us. They gathered for the Feast of Pentecost and had an experience they described as *"a sound like the rush of a mighty wind"* (Acts 2:2), and it filled the entire house where they were sitting. There appeared to them tongues of fire, distributed and resting on each one of them, and they were all filled with the Holy Spirit. This was evident to others and many joined their fellowship. The community grew.

For a time, there were people in the early churches who could tell about Jesus from personal experience. As these began to die off, there was a need to have their recollections written down to preserve them. The four Gospels of Mark, Luke, Matthew and John provide information about Jesus. They tell the story from different viewpoints, but it is evident in all four of them that Jesus demonstrated the mystery of a living relationship with God.

The gospel of Mark was written some forty years after the crucifixion. It begins with an account of Jesus being baptized, tells of his healing and teaching, and concludes with the women finding his tomb empty.

The next two gospels of Matthew and Luke were written around sixty to seventy years after the crucifixion. Matthew and Luke also provide genealogies that trace Jesus' lineage from his father Joseph back through generations that include King David and Abraham, all the way to Adam, who is called the son of God. These lists in Matthew and Luke sometimes deviate from each other, but both show Jesus as descended from David through Jesus' father Joseph.

Matthew's gospel begins by stating that Jesus is *"the son of David, the son of Abraham"* (Matthew 1:1), followed by a list of descendants from Abraham to David, then from David to Joseph the father of Jesus. Gospel writers emphasized a lineage from David which could identify Jesus as the expected Messiah (see Apocalyptic above). They called him Christ, which means Messiah in the Greek language.

Matthew tells the story of the birth of Jesus this way: *"When his mother Mary had been betrothed to Joseph, before they came together she was found to be with child... Joseph, being a just man and unwilling to put her to shame, resolved to divorce her quietly"* (Matthew 1:18–19).

Joseph did not follow the law which said that a woman found to have lost her virginity before marriage was to be stoned. This act of putting compassion before the written law was obviously considered by the writer to be the mark of a just man. Jesus was raised in the household of Joseph, a Jew who put compassion before obedience to strict scriptural laws. This was the example of fatherhood Jesus knew in his childhood. There may have been many types of fathers in that society, but this just man was the father Jesus had known when he called God "Father."

Luke's account of Jesus' birth gives more details of Mary being impregnated by the Holy Spirit, journeying to Bethlehem to give birth, and angels telling shepherds about it.

Matthew's gospel relates the visit of the Magi to see the infant Jesus and the king's attempt to kill him, which occasioned the child being taken to Egypt to escape. Luke tells that baby Jesus was baptized and taken to Nazareth where he grew up and went to the Jerusalem Passover with his family at age twelve.

Matthew tells of Jesus giving a sermon on a mountain. Both Matthew and Luke recount many healing occasions, parables, and an account of Jesus' trial and crucifixion. Both tell of women finding the tomb empty and the resurrected Jesus giving his disciples a mandate to *"make disciples of all nations... teaching them to observe all that I have commanded you and lo, I am with you always"* (Matthew 28:19–20).

These three gospels differ, as accounts of an event told by several people usually do. They reveal the spirit in which Jesus taught and acted and are nearer the facts of Jesus' life than John's Gospel, which was written a hundred years after the crucifixion.

By this time, the community had come to some conclusions about Jesus. John begins by saying, *"The word was with God and the word was God"* (John 1:1). Word is the English translation of the Greek word *logos*, which means focused and ordered thought. Then John says, *"All things were made through him and without him was not anything made that was made"* (John 1:3). Without God's ordered thought, this amazingly organized planet would not have come into being. John states that Jesus is the *logos* made flesh. By personifying the *logos* as Jesus, John declares that Jesus existed from the beginning of creation. Evidence of a person's ordered thought reveals the sort of person they are. John says this with, *"No one has ever seen God. The only Son who is in the bosom of the father, he has made him known"* (John 1:18).

John also says, *"In him was light and the light was the life of men"* (John 1:4). Here John uses the Persian concept of light to communicate with literate people of that day that Jesus is the light of the world. John's intent is clearly stated several chapters later: *"These are written that you may believe that Jesus is the Christ [Messiah], the Son of God and that believing you may have life in his name"* (John 20:31).

John tells of Jesus personally, declaring who he is in statements such as, *"I am the bread of life"* (John 6:35), *"I am the light of the world"* (John 9:5), *"I am the good shepherd"* (John 10:11), *"I am the resurrection and the life"* (John 11:25), *"I am the way, the truth and the life"* (John 14:6), and *"I am the true vine"* (John 15:1).

These statements have Jesus affirming the mystery which the community later sensed in him. This differs from the other three gospels, in which Jesus says things like, *"Why do you call me good? No one is good but God alone"* (Mark 10:18, Luke 18:19). John uses narrative and symbolism to communicate the faith of the early church. His gospel has many nicely phrased devotional passages that are easily memorized, and these have inspired Christian people for centuries.

CHAPTER SIX

The First Christian Communities

Jesus' followers gathered together on the Day of Pentecost and had a common experience of God which they interpreted as the Holy Spirit. Others joined them and the community grew. They tried to help each other live the faith Jesus had taught them by word and example, and were called those *"belonging to the Way"* (Acts 9:2). That Spirit of being the people of Jesus' way has been at the core of Christianity ever since, despite various forces of history and intellectual theories that have at various times overlaid or twisted it.

A Pharisee named Saul felt that this community should be forcefully discouraged. He set out for Damascus, intending to use violence against followers of Jesus. Then something surprising happened! While bent on violence, Saul experienced the very thing he sought to destroy, which changed him dramatically.

Saul was blinded until he was received by a representative of the local church; then his eyes were opened. He writes, *"I went away into Arabia"* (Galatians 1:17), a desert country. Similar to Jesus going to his baptism to spend time in the wilderness, Saul returned believing that Jesus was the Son of God.

Saul changed his name to Paul and devoted the remainder of his life to helping the Christian movement grow. He traveled widely and preached in Jewish synagogues that Jesus is the son of God. He formed groups that became followers of Jesus and called these groups churches. After moving on, he wrote letters to these churches. These letters, called epistles, became part of the New Testament. Paul also preached to Gentiles, and his way of interpreting Jesus was significant in expanding the Christian movement beyond its original Jewish base.

Let us pause and think back.

Remember the exile during which the Jews, under duress, developed gatherings that developed into synagogues, which Paul could use to tell his message about Jesus.

Remember the battles between Greek empires that drove many Jews to leave their homeland and form Jewish settlements with synagogues in many other countries—available for Paul to take his message beyond Israel.

Remember the Greek empire that required the use of the Greek language throughout all the Mediterranean area—a common language that enabled literate people in many countries to read Paul's letters and other Christian literature.

Remember the power of Rome stopping the wars and establishing protection for travelers. Paul was safer in his travels and able to appeal to Rome when the Jews arrested him.

Ask yourself, was God working in all this history to prepare the way for the Christian message?

As we begin to look at what the Christian movement taught, it is important to be aware that God's people have always used their experiences to shape their mental concepts of God. Remember the pillars of cloud and fire in the wilderness, the tabernacle made of poles and curtains, the Ark of the Covenant and the temple. These served their purpose, in their time and context, but they were left behind as circumstance changed. The mystery of God was the reality that lived on.

We shall look next at the concepts and theories that Christians have generated to carry and communicate their sense of the mystery of Jesus. We need to be aware that these theories are shaped by their environments. They are a sort of packaging for Christianity, but it is the mystery of Jesus' spirit that they are trying to convey. The theories should be continually assessed to determine how adequately or poorly they convey his spirit.

There is sometimes a need to repair some packaging of Christianity or replace it. Generally, some people will always want to hold on to the old and familiar, like wanting to keep the old hand pump because they don't trust modern plumbing. We need to remember that the refreshment is not in the pump, nor the plumbing, but in the spring of water.

Living with the mystery that is God, you can watch or participate in adjustments to theories and forms of worship or language without stress, because they are not the essence. We can find fellowship with people who relate to the mystery, even if they package it in concepts that are different from ours.

As I proceed to consider the development of thinking in Christianity, I will draw your attention to some of the flaws in the way Christianity has been packaged. Bear in mind that this is not in any sense being negative toward the mystery that is Christianity.

Followers of Jesus felt in him the love of God and the forgiveness of God. Paul encouraged *"forgiving one another, as God in Christ forgave you"* (Ephesians 4:32). This and other passages refer to forgiveness as being a common experience in Christ's presence. Jesus' followers simply rejoiced in this and tried to live the love he had shown.

People who believed the theory that God plans all things looked for a tidy formula to explain why God would plan such a cruel death for his son. Jewish temple worship had insisted that an unblemished sacrifice be offered before God could forgive. These two theories brought people to the conclusion that the forgiveness Christians were experiencing must have meant that a sacrifice without blemish had been made. Jesus was considered without blemish, so they concluded his death was the needed sacrifice.

This theory is explained in Hebrews 9:12—*"He entered once for all into the Holy Place taking not the blood of goats and calves but his own blood, thus securing an eternal redemption"*—and Hebrews 9:14—*"If the sprinkling of defiled persons with the blood of goats and bulls… sanctifies for the purification of the flesh, how much more shall the blood of Christ who through the eternal spirit offered himself without blemish to God, purify your conscience."* Hebrews 10:14 states, *"By a single offering he has perfected for all time those who are sanctified."*

This epistle was addressed to Hebrews (Jews). The first Christian community consisted of Jews who were familiar with the system of the temple whereby *"under the law, almost everything is purified with blood"* (Hebrews 9:22). Jews thus had a basis for accepting this interpretation of the crucifixion.

This theory has been widely accepted in Christianity, but it distorts the meaning of sacrifice. Sacrifice involves offering something one values as a symbol of offering oneself. Abraham's willingness to sacrifice Isaac was an extreme example of his loyalty to God, and carried no suggestion that it bought forgiveness of sin. Giving a sacrifice is a concrete way of offering oneself in love. The death of Jesus Christ can be seen as a concrete expression of God giving his son as a gift of love, whether or not he was crucified.

Most worship services today draw upon this element of sacrifice through offering by which the worshiper gives something of value to symbolize offering one's life to God. In our culture, the valued object is generally money. Offering money in order to get any sort of reward makes the act of giving like a business investment. Offering money to get forgiveness makes the act of giving a bribe. Either one dilutes the act of loving dedication. A real sacrifice is always given without expecting rewards.

In a more primitive civilization, the valued object would be an animal, and it would be killed to make the offering final. Leviticus 6:25–26 states, *"This is the law of the sin offering… The Priest who offers it shall eat it… every male among the priests may eat of it."* I suspect that the temple priests promoted this theory of earning forgiveness through sacrifice as an appeal to a self-serving instinct in the worshipers. This theory might encourage more sacrifices, which would mean more meat for the priests.

In Luke 15:11–32, Jesus tells a story known as the parable of the Prodigal Son. In this parable, the younger son wasted his father's generosity but was nonetheless forgiven freely and joyfully. The parable also includes a conversation between the father and his elder son, who was offended that no sacrifice had been required before his younger brother was forgiven. The father explains that forgiveness was given because of love and assures the elder brother that he, too, was loved and invited to share in celebrating the return of the wayward brother.

In this parable, Jesus used the example of a father with a wayward son to reveal the nature of God. His hearers would have been quite conscious of his meaning. Jesus made it clear that God receives with joy the sinful one who repents, and does not withhold forgiveness until someone has made appropriate sacrifice. God invites his people to do likewise. Knowing they are loved, God's people can be glad to see a person who has been bad changing for the better. They may not throw a party, but they can offer support to help him or her find a new attitude to life.

I do not believe that God would be so limited in his capacity to forgive that he would have to arrange the evil of a crucifixion. Who or what is God obliged to placate? There is no higher authority than God. This theory has appealed to an instinct to get something in return for accepting Christ; it may have brought people into the Christian movement, but it is not logical and portrays God in a way that is contrary to Jesus. It denies Jesus' revelation that God forgives because he loves.

Jesus' death and resurrection touched the hearts of people and moved them to find in him a revelation of God that is life-transforming. Jesus thus encourages people to be all that they were created to be and not a lesser version of their potential. In this sense, Jesus can be seen as Saviour. The fact that he was crucified has been key to eliciting this response, rather than to placating God.

WHO IS JESUS?

People in those early churches looked for an explanation about who Jesus was and the nature of his relationship to God. Their experience in that culture was that a person's status depended on who his parents were. Only the son of a king could be a king, and the son of a king was royal by birth. Kings who wished to exert royal presence in an area of their kingdom would send a son. The people would recognize that in the presence of the king's son, the king's authority was with them. Early Christians felt the presence of God in their relationship to Jesus, so they explained the mystery of God's presence being with Jesus by saying that Jesus was the son of God.

Tracing the ancestry of Jesus through many generations shows that Jesus was descended from David through his father, Joseph. This was to give credence to the theory that Jesus could be the expected Messiah. That was not enough for some, so we find these same two gospels, Matthew and Luke, also tell about God impregnating a virgin, making the son born of this conception the biological son of God. These narratives also show Jesus as not Joseph's son, and therefore not descended from David, and thus not the Messiah. However, these are romantic stories that are easily remembered and have provided a basis for the faith of many people.

The early Christians and countless people over many generations have believed in the virgin birth, and called Jesus the Christ or Messiah. The two theories do not fit together. This is not logical, but attempts to express the mystery.

The Gospel of Mark was written more than twenty years closer to the events being described than Matthew or Luke, and introduces Jesus as a young man who turns up at a revival led by John the Baptist. This marks the first report of Jesus' first appearance in public, and is probably as close to the historical facts as we may come. I believe God has come in Jesus and whatever process was involved is a mystery we cannot know.

Paul's letters were written thirty years closer to the events of Jesus' life than Matthew and Luke. Paul sees Jesus' authenticity as being grounded in his descent from David and by God's having resurrected him and thereby designated him Son of God in power. Paul states this in his epistle to the Romans: *"Jesus Christ…who was descended from David according to the flesh and designated son of God in power according to the Spirit of holiness by his resurrection from the dead"* (Romans 1:1–4). Paul doesn't mention a virgin birth.

The written word of scripture was altered by Jews in a specific way when read in the synagogue, and this may have contributed to ideas about Jesus. The *"I am who I am"* (Exodus 3:14) that was told to Moses as God's name was written in Hebrew with four letters whose equivalents in English would be *y h w h*. This was the name of God to be found in Hebrew Scriptures. Later, Israelites took the commandment "You shall not take the name of God in vain" so literally that they dared not speak yhwh aloud. Accordingly, when the reader reading the scriptures in the synagogue encountered yhwh in the text, he would say Adonai, which means "The Lord."

The Hebrew written language uses only consonants. With yhwh not said aloud, the sound of the word was lost over time. When Hebrew scriptures were later translated into other languages, the word yhwh was written as THE LORD, in uppercase, to indicate that this is not the real word, but is what the reader was to say aloud when he encountered yhwh in the text. You can find this in the King James Version of the Bible. Some modern versions say Yahweh, which is only their guess. Others write YHWH to indicate that yhwh cannot be pronounced.

The disciples were students of Jesus and they sometimes called him teacher. When he was not physically present, they might refer to him as the Lord. After his resurrection, it became common in the early churches to refer to Jesus as the Lord Jesus Christ. People accustomed to speaking of God as the Lord could easily come to think of the Lord Jesus as God.

Complications with this raise questions. Could the mystery behind the whole world walk around in Palestine for a few years? If Jesus is God, to whom did he pray? What meaning could there be in many quotes of Jesus such as, *"For I have come down from heaven, not to do my own will, but the will of him who sent me"* (John 6:38), and in Gethsemane, *"My father, if it be possible let this cup pass from me, nevertheless not as I will but as you will"* (Matthew 26:39). Or from the cross: *"My God why hast thou forsaken me?"* (Matthew 27:46) and *"Father, into thy hands I commit my spirit"* (Luke 23:46).

People in the early church developed different ways of talking about how Jesus related to God. Some said he was the son of God. Others said he was God. Some said he existed from the beginning and others said he was born of Mary and only became the son of God at his resurrection. They developed complicated theories to defend their positions. Some said the spirit they knew was God's spirit, others that it was Christ's spirit. Others said the spirit was a separate entity. These issues were debated passionately, yet all held the basic belief that God was revealed in Jesus.

I believe Christians can see Jesus as the son of God, in whom the presence of God can be known, without settling specifics about his conception or his royal lineage. Birth stories of Jesus may have sentimental value, and Messianic theories may support calling Jesus the Christ, but they both point to mystery rather than historical fact. I believe that God has come in Jesus and whatever process was involved is a mystery we cannot know.

CHAPTER SEVEN

The Catholic Church

When a Roman emperor decided to adopt Christianity, he ordered Christians to get together and agree in order that there be one firm belief he could impose on his people. He expected Christianity to be a source of unity in the empire. A council of bishops was called to establish one faith that the whole body of Christians believed. After long deliberation, they produced a statement that said God was one, yet three persons—Father, Son and Holy Ghost.

The bishops stated that this faith in Trinity was according to what the whole Christian people believed. The Greek preface for "according to" is *kata* and the word for "whole" is *holos*, so they called this the *kata holic*, or catholic, faith. The church became known as the Catholic Church.

The eastern portion of the Church, with its capital at Constantinople on the Black Sea, did not agree with their interpretation of Christ and split off to become the Eastern Orthodox Church with its head a Patriarch instead of a Pope. They used the Greek language instead of Latin. This Orthodox Church spread north and eastward into Central Europe and Russia and eventually came with immigrants from those countries to North America.

The protection of the Roman Empire provided the Catholic Church with an opportunity to convert whole populations in Europe to Christianity. This meant that the Church had to deal with the fact that these were people who did not have the Jewish background of faith in God. Many of the theories and practices of the Catholic Church developed from the Church trying to fit the Christian message into non-Jewish patterns of thinking already familiar to these people.

One of the factors of these people not having a Jewish background was that they did not feel any need for sacrifice to obtain forgiveness. The sacrifice theory did not speak to them. They did have a sense of guilt, however, and the Church taught them that God would apply the suffering of Christ to those sins that were confessed to a priest. This provided people with a valuable opportunity to divulge their guilt in confidence to another person, who would listen carefully and offer a way to deal with it.

Powerful rulers felt that allowing any infraction of their rule to go unpunished would be seen as weakness by their people. This made a ruler feel he could not forgive without losing credibility, unless he kept the public afraid by punishing a substitute. Thinkers applied this to Christianity and taught that Jesus was punished as a substitute so that God could forgive our sins. People beyond Judaism could accept this theory, because they saw it as simply the way kings or rulers acted.

The intent was to give significance to Jesus and his crucifixion, but this theory interprets God as being limited to the essentially self-serving, unjust methods used by powerful rulers. I do not believe God is limited as these rulers were. God, as revealed in and by Jesus Christ, simply would not devise a scheme to inflict this sort of injustice on an innocent person.

Nonetheless, this was accepted by people of that day and has still been accepted in recent years by many who would never approve of that sort of justice in a government. It is not Christianity, but a way of packaging Christianity which is dated. And it is definitely not part of my faith.

During the recent war in Kosovo, a man who had grown up in that country was discussing the tendency for violence in that corner of the world. I asked him what he felt could be the solution and he said, "Look, if your grandfather killed my grandfather, then I have to kill you, and some day your grandson will have to kill my grandson. That's just the way it is. There is no solution."

There probably is no solution, if you believe that even God holds people guilty for the sins of their ancestors and cannot forgive unless someone suffers. I believe that in Christ there is a solution.

In Matthew 5:44–45, Jesus gives the radical command, *"Love your enemies and pray for those who persecute you, so that you may be sons of your Father who is in heaven; for he makes the sun rise on the evil and on the good, and sends rain on the just and on the unjust."*

Jesus' prayer tells us to ask the heavenly father to *"forgive us our sins, for we ourselves forgive every one who is indebted to us"* (Luke 11:4). Jesus' view of forgiveness is that forgiveness received relates to forgiveness given. This is distinctive of Jesus. There is no suggestion that some other innocent person must suffer in order for the sin, debt, or trespass to be forgiven.

Another practice of rulers in that day was to seize someone who had friends with resources and imprison this person until a ransom was paid. Some used this idea to teach that the devil held the whole human race in his power and would not release them unless he was paid a ransom. They taught that God gave his only son as a ransom for the freedom of humans from domination by the devil. Matthew and Mark both say, *"The son of man came not to be served but to serve and to give his life a ransom for many"* (Matthew 20:28, Mark 10:45).

This ransom theory had the advantage of not seeing God as being behind the scheme. This theory rests on belief in a devil, and was not as widely accepted as those of sacrifice or substitution, so you may not have heard of it. I mention it because the latter two theories were not the only ones formulated by the early Church.

People who went to great lengths to avoid sin were taught that they were lost anyway, because Adam sinned and every human being inherited Adam's guilt. A variation on this theory was the theory of original sin. This one says God created a perfect human race, but there was a fall, illustrated by the story of Adam and Eve. The theory goes that Eve, being tempted by a snake, coaxed Adam to go along and the two of them disobeyed God. This was the original sin, after which their children and all descendants were believed to inherit original sin and thus need to be saved.

I do not believe this. The idea that evil is innate in people suggests that evil is normal behaviour and removes the incentive to cease to do evil. I believe evil is not part of being human, but arises through misdirection of good and natural urges. Appropriate fulfillment for these urges has a pattern which generally takes time and patience. Evil generally enters if the soul reaches for a faster way that does damage to others or itself.

Absolute human rulers punished disrespect or disobedience with horrible tortures, so Christian leaders assumed God would also. They imagined that souls in hell would be burned with fire and they would have to endure this forever.

This teaching about hell has contributed to the fear of death. The Roman Catholic Church provided many procedures one could follow to avoid going to hell. Protestant churches taught that the only essential doctrine was believing that Christ died for sin. Both of these methods provided a strong incentive to become

Christian. Sending missionaries to people in newly discovered countries was often inspired by concern to save them from being sent to hell.

One day, I was visiting parishioners in a Brockville hospital when a nurse asked me to call on a man who was in great pain, although he was not identified with my church. He was indeed suffering very much and appreciated my visit. When I asked him if he would like me to pray with him, he said, "You do whatever you damn well please, but I do not believe any of that stuff about God." As I was leaving, though, he said he would like me to come back.

I did call on him regularly for several weeks. Being with him in his pain seemed to help him—a mystery I believed was God's love flowing through me, but he wouldn't have used those terms. I was with him when he died, and I thanked God that he was finally free of his pain.

As I walked out of that hospital, I realized something. This man did not believe any of the things Christian theology said he needed to believe in order to avoid hell, but I was sure God would not send him to where he would have more pain.

In that moment outside the Brockville hospital, I realized very clearly that I definitely did not believe in hell.

Using the word hell as a forceful way to talk about someone having to endure great pain or difficulty is quite different from believing a theory that God sends people to hell after we die. The great prophets taught that wrong conduct can bring consequences, but they meant here in this life.

Scriptures written before the Persian experience have much to say about evil, but do not mention hell or a devil. The book of Genesis mentions a snake in the Garden of Eden, not a devil. It is only in scriptures written after the Persian experience that there is mention of a devil and a multitude of evil spirits.

The theory of hell and a devil was added to the thinking of the people of God from a Persian source, but is not part of the faith that began with Moses, expanded in the Ten Commandments, the law, the teaching of the great prophets and the spirit of Jesus Christ. It has no place in my faith.

Jesus Christ reveals God as desiring that we should fulfill the potential we were created for. The objective of life is not to avoid hell, but to live with God, for God, and thus know wholeness (holiness) in our souls. Christ taught people to let go of past injury and live together in harmony, whether in the home, the community or the planet.

Forgiveness is not ignoring the wrong, nor diminishing its significance. Love may need to be firm to name the sin and take action to stop what is damaging people, but Christian love gets no satisfaction in seeing the offender or anybody else getting punished.

Before Christianity was accepted by Rome, the first Christians had been severely persecuted, and despite the fact that some had endured terrible tortures, they refused to reject Christ. There was a strong feeling among Christians that those who had not suffered should not get the same reward of heaven as those who had endured for their faith. It seemed to them that there was an injustice if everyone got the same reward when some had suffered more than others.

The Catholic Church got around this worry by teaching that all confessing Christians would go to heaven, but the martyrs would go to heaven immediately. Those who had not suffered would go to a place called purgatory, where they would be purged of any residual sin before getting into heaven.

Purgatory would be unpleasant, but the church taught that special services and prayers for the dead could influence God to reduce their time in purgatory. The bereaved were therefore provided with something they could do to help their dead loved ones.

Human rulers at that time were not exposed to the public without being surrounded by soldiers and advisors. An ordinary person would have little chance of getting near a monarch. They needed someone to speak for them who would have a better chance of influencing the king.

Patterns from their experience with rulers influenced the way people thought about God. Therefore, they believed that those who had been especially devout would have more influence with God to grant miracles. The Church gave such people the title of saints, and people could pray to them, asking them to use their influence with God. Jesus was also believed to intercede with God for us.

Think of a primitive religion (above) that emphasizes looking for ways we may influence God to do what we want, instead of focusing on doing what God made us for. I believe God deals with each of us in love without us needing anyone to ask God for favours.

New Christians were baptized to express a relationship to Jesus, who was baptized. It was seen as symbolic of the beginning of a new life. The Catholic Church taught that one could not go to heaven unless one was baptized, so people began having infants baptized. This raised the question of what happened to an infant who died without being baptized.

They reasoned that infants were innocent of any sin, but should they die without baptism, the theory of Adam's sin would keep them out of heaven. To resolve this worry, the Catholic Church introduced another gradation of afterlife that was not heaven, not hell, and not purgatory. They taught that the soul of an infant who did not get baptized would go to limbo.

Let us think about that one. To suggest that God's love for an infant must be subject to a rite of the church limits God and is far from the spirit of Christ. This theory was a way of solving a problem that arose from combining the theory that all are tainted by Adam's sin with the theory that a lack of words and rites of the church could keep God from expressing his love. This problem illustrates the absurdity of both these theories.

The Catholic Church was unwilling to give up either of these theories, and so invented a third theory called limbo with a further problem. Jesus said, *"Let the children come to me and do not hinder them; for to such belongs the kingdom of heaven"* (Matthew 19:14). Would Jesus endorse sending any child to such a place as limbo?

The Protestant reformers rejected this theory about limbo. For them, baptizing a baby was a powerful affirmation that God loved the child and received him or her before the child could do anything to earn it. Later Protestant groups believed that according to the Bible, babies should not be baptized, only persons who could make a profession of their faith in Jesus Christ, and always by complete immersion.

I believe the sacrament of baptism, whether by sprinkling or immersion, for babies or adults, is a commitment by all persons involved to a responsibility before God to be faithful in nourishing faith. God is not limited by whether or not some rite is performed or how much water is employed.

Some saw the story of Adam and Eve as revealing sex to be the original sin. This suggests that all persons born from a conception that involved sexual activity are born with original sin. The human race is therefore "fallen"—all men are sinners. The virgin birth story has Jesus conceived with no sex involved, portraying Jesus as the only human without blemish—without original sin. All others are thereby seen as in need of the Grace of Jesus Christ, administered, of course, by the Catholic Church. This, too, is merely a packaging of Christianity.

Many people were led to feel that sex is sinful and therefore prevents personal holiness. Some men tried to be very holy by embracing a lifestyle of avoiding sex. They were called monks, and formed communities called monasteries, in which this way of life was practiced. Some women took up the same life-style and formed communities called convents.

These communities not only lived a life of prayer, but some established hospitals for the sick and orphanages for children or welfare for the poor. They preserved and copied the Bible and educated priests. These activities and the prayer of Francis of Assisi indicate that despite being based on illogical theory, the spirit of Christ had an effect.

There were also devout men who lived this celibate life in ordinary society. These were called friars, and people often considered them more religious than the priests who were married. Many would turn to a friar rather than a priest for religious ceremonies. To reclaim the respect of the people, the Bishop of Rome (by now called the Pope) required that all priests be celibate. This rejection of sex became a requirement for clergy, a prac-tice that still continues in the Roman Catholic Church.

I do not believe in equating sex with sin. This sug-gests that God made a mistake in creating sex. In scrip-ture, the commandment "You shall not commit adul-tery" does not forbid sex. It requires strict sexual faith-fulness to one partner. God created men and women with sexual attraction for one another and committed exclusive relationship as the place for fulfillment of this desire.

God designed this as a place wherein children can be born and raised to fulfill their potential as men and women. Human cultures may call it marriage or some other designation, and most shape some ritual to establish it publically as permanent. These customs may change, but God's purpose does not change and is essential for continuing human life.

To require celibacy of clergy implies that marriage is less acceptable to God than celibacy and that priests are of a different nature than ordinary people. I don't believe in either idea. Celibate clergy are prevented from experiencing the joys and responsibilities of family life that could enable them to better empathize with parishioners.

While I doubt the wisdom of a celibate clergy, I do recognize that many of these clergy fulfill a role that has helped many individuals to know the spirit of Jesus. When a movement to reform the Catholic Church appeared, it was clergy that proposed it, and often suffered for it.

The Catholic Church developed a system of specific practices that included regular attendance at mass, fasting on Fridays, observance of saint's days, penance and pilgrimages. These gave individuals a means to make ongoing concrete expressions of faith, and to nourish their relationship with God. Such opportunities are valuable but diluted if they are tied to assurances that hell is thereby being avoided and time in purgatory kept to a minimum.

The Catholic Church became aware of ideas and practices that were already familiar to people in the culture into which it was spreading, and provided Christian interpretations for these.

There was one ancient custom that was valued by many northern countries. During a certain period of each year, the days got shorter and darkness seemed to overcome light. People were aware that there was a point at which the advance of darkness was stopped and the daylight began to get longer. This occasioned a big celebration. In most northern countries, this celebration became part of their primitive religion.

The Catholic Church declared that this celebration was a recognition of Jesus' birth and called it Christmas. No one knows exactly when Jesus was born, but around the winter solstice is a good time to celebrate his coming. Over the centuries, Christmas has encouraged the mystery of generosity in many people.

The Catholic Church adopted the Roman Empire's style of organization. The empire had one emperor over all, while the Church had a Pope. The empire then had governors who supervised each area and were responsible to the emperor. The Church had bishops who supervised the churches in an area and were responsible to the Pope. The empire had army officers who were responsible for the peace of the general public in the governor's area and followed his orders. The church had priests responsible for the spiritual welfare of the people in the bishop's area, and who took orders from the bishop.

This centralization of authority in one individual is used in business and military organizations. With this efficient system, the Roman Empire dominated the Mediterranean area and much of Europe, and the Roman

Catholic Church used the same efficiency to dominate Christianity in the same area. It had the disadvantage of tempting its leaders to use power in ways that may not have furthered the spirit of Jesus.

In the onward march of history, Germanic peoples from Central Europe overran the Roman Empire, causing a breakdown of central government. Europe broke up into feudal systems with local lords each protecting and controlling the people in their area. This left the Catholic Church as the only system that was unified across the continent, which increased its power with the people.

Loss of the Roman Empire's protection left the Catholic Church having to deal with multiple secular powers and caused it to become involved in power struggles between kings and princely powers. Popes were suspected of corruption, which eventually caused dissatisfaction and unrest in the Church.

CHAPTER EIGHT

The Protestant Reformation

Pressure for reform arose within the Church itself. Monasteries taught Catholic clergy to read, and this enabled them to discover in the Bible that much of what was happening in the Catholic Church was not in harmony with Jesus' spirit. This convinced them that they should do something about it. Many individuals tried to persuade the Church to change its teachings and practices where they deviated from the teaching and spirit of Christ. Popes perceived any reform as a threat to their power, however, and made deals with secular leaders to put down change with force. Reformers were persecuted and some were killed.

People who believe they have the only truth can also believe that any deviation from that truth constitutes a challenge to the will of God. These beliefs can turn into a conviction that they would be serving God by using deadly means to silence any who promote differing viewpoints. We can see this sequence at work in the motivation of the Pharisees and Sadducees arranging to have the secular authority of Rome kill Jesus, in the motivation of Saul planning to silence the first Christians at Damascus, and in the motivation of Roman Catholic popes arranging to have secular rulers persecute and kill the first reformers.

Eventually, a monk named Martin Luther made up a list of things in the Catholic Church that he considered unbiblical and nailed this list to a church door in October 1517. The Catholic Church authorities threatened him. Frederick, Elector of Saxony, was Luther's sovereign and defended Luther. Under this prince's protection, Luther's teachings spread and many developed a desire to have the Church reformed.

Kings of nations in the north of Europe had been restless about the power being exerted over their people by a leader in Italy. Luther's teaching gave them justification for reforming the churches in their countries and thus taking their people away from the power of the Pope.

Popes rallied other nations to send armies to stop this movement, which was now called Protestantism. Much of Europe was thus drawn into a war over the way Christianity should be expressed.

It should be noted that so-called religious wars were not about Christianity, but about the way cultures were packaging Christianity. The more faith gets focused on theories and religious structures, instead of the mystery, the greater the risk of things turning violent.

In this case, the fighting went on for years. The Lutheran Church survived this struggle and went with German or Scandinavian people wherever they settled.

In France, a priest named John Calvin became convinced that the Christian Church should conform to what was in the Bible. In 1534, he published a book outlining his interpretations of Christianity according to the Bible. Such teaching put him in danger, so he moved to Switzerland. The Pope could not persuade kings to send armies into that mountainous country to stop him. He continued to teach his understanding of the Bible and reformed the Church in Switzerland.

The reform movement had the Bible translated from the original Greek and Hebrew into the languages of the people. The objective was to change Christian authority from a pope who had been seen as having authority from God, to seeing the Bible as the very words of God.

Luther removed from the Church everything he felt the Bible rejected and kept the rest. Calvin taught that nothing should be in the Church that was not advocated in the Bible, yet Calvinist churches kept the trinity and infant baptism, which are not mentioned in the Bible.

Calvinism emphasized the sovereignty of God to the extent that Calvin believed God to have planned everything in advance. This theory was called predestination. People found a sense of stability in believing that whatever was happening was God's plan. This made difficulties easier for them to accept and to endure.

Predestination taught that every person's life was already planned by God, who had established what they would do or believe, so that God expected you to be good, but had already planned that you would. This theory was humbling, in that you could not expect credit for your good works, because you would be humbly doing what God had predestined you to do.

Calvinists did not mention that this logic would also mean one should not expect punishment for doing bad things, because this, too, was apparently what God planned. God was being portrayed as sending persons to hell for doing what he had predestined them to do. It harmonizes with a theory that God has already chosen who would be saved and who would be damned.

I do not believe the theory of predestination or the bundle of ideas that spring from it. This is not the nature of God that Jesus reveals. I believe your soul is free to make its own decisions and responsible to recognize they have consequences, in the dimensions of your soul as well as in more visible manners. Living with God means taking responsibility for what you do.

Each of us needs to know that God created us with capacity to care about others, to be helpful and not damaging to others or the things they depend on. We all need to be helped to have a vision of who we can be and encouraged to pursue that vision. This is a function of Christianity.

Calvin developed a church system which had ordained persons who were not called priests, but preaching elders. These shared administrative responsibilities with a court of elders, who were laymen elected by the local people in the congregation, and made decisions together, sitting in a court called Session.

The Bishop's function of supervising congregations in an area was given to a court of elders who were appointed by local sessions. The Greek word for elder was *presbyter*, so the supervising court was called a Presbytery. Eventually, the preaching elders came to be called ministers and were ordained by the court of Presbytery. This type of church was called Presbyterian.

The Reformed or Presbyterian Church spread to Holland, Scotland, and wherever Dutch or Scottish people settled. The Presbyterian Church was governed by courts made up of persons who were chosen for that purpose by the people in the church. This planted ideas that eventually grew into democracies in much of Europe.

Since Presbyterian theology was not considered unchangeable, ideas about predestination mellowed as people began to think more logically. Calvinism developed into a Presbyterian Church that nourishes people in their relationship with God, encourages them to express the love of God in their dealings with people, and provides a means of working together on projects for the common good.

Reform groups were developed in France and called Huguenots. Catherine De Medicos, wife of Henry II of France and mother of the next three French kings, organized to have each Catholic identify a Calvinist neighbour and plan to kill that Huguenot.

This was to be done all together on the same day, so reprisal would have to deal with so many individuals that it would be impractical. On St. Bartholomew's Day,

1572, six thousand Huguenot were killed. That huge massacre caused most remaining Huguenot to leave France, with the result that France remained mostly Roman Catholic. People in other countries who have a French background tend to be Roman Catholic.

In England, King Henry VIII wanted a divorce from his first wife, but it was denied him by the Pope. Henry declared that the King of England was head of the English Church and it was therefore free from the Pope. Then Henry divorced his wife, but insisted on maintaining Catholic practices in the Church of England. English clergy, now freed from the Pope, started thinking of reforming the church. When Henry died, the next king was only a boy and he allowed reform to progress in the English church. That boy king died in a few years without heir.

Mary, daughter of Henry's first wife and granddaughter of the king of Spain, became queen. She revoked Henry's decree, restoring the English Church to Rome. She had the clergy who had pushed for reform publically repent or be killed by burning. Many died and others fled the country.

At that time, most of Europe was involved in war over religion, so the only safe place for English clergy to go was Switzerland. John Calvin was teaching the Bible there, so these refugee clergy studied under him.

When Queen Mary died and Elizabeth (daughter of Henry's second wife) became queen, the Pope did not recognize Henry's divorce and said that Elizabeth was illegitimate. If she recognized the authority of the Pope, her right to be queen would be questioned. She declared that she, as the Queen of England, was head of the English Church and the Pope had no jurisdiction there.

The English clergy came home from Switzerland convinced that Calvin was right and spread his ideas in England. Many people were convinced and became eager for reform. Church leaders saw that there were many people in England who valued the Catholic connection, but also those who were strongly for reform. The bishops decided that the Church of England would have a form of worship and structure that would be acceptable to both Catholics and Protestants.

Queen Elizabeth I saw that most of Europe was caught up in war over religion and that there was danger of the conflict spreading into England. Elizabeth therefore authorized the compromise. Disputes over the design of Christianity in England settled down and the Church of England continues to have this middle-of-the-road form to this day.

Some people in England continued to be passionate for purifying the Church and were called Puritans. These were persecuted, so they crossed the Atlantic to settle in what was then British North America. Other people in England felt that each congregation should be free to govern its own affairs and choose their own understandings. These people were called Congregationalists, and some of them crossed to North America and became the Congregational Church.

English settlement in North America brought the Church of England with them, calling it the Anglican

Church. The revolution that produced the United States of America made the Anglican name unacceptable in that country, so the name was changed to the Episcopalian Church. This church in the United States still has elements of both Catholic and Protestant practice, but it does not recognize the Queen of England as its head.

Note that royalty in England manipulated the packaging of Christianity in that country for personal or political reasons, but the mystery of Jesus' spirit continued and the compromise of Catholic and Protestant packaging has worked. The Anglican Church came to Canada with English settlers. It nourishes relationship to God, and the spirit of Jesus is expressed in its people.

The Industrial Revolution changed the pattern of population in England. Manufacturing caused cities to grow as rural people moved there to work in factories. Far away from their local churches and communities, many of these people lost contact with Christianity.

John Wesley, a Church of England priest, was concerned about these people. He preached to them at factory and mine gates, and converted many to active Christian faith. He developed a method of nourishing their faith in groups that were called Methodist Societies. This movement was more concerned with the mystery than with church structure and grew apart from the Church of England to become the Methodist Church.

The Methodist Church was not identified with any specific nationality, but expanded in the United States and Canada by holding revival events at which people of all backgrounds were converted. These were brought into a fellowship of living in the spirit of Jesus that helped individuals develop dimensions of their soul. Methodism also promoted changes in their society designed to serve human needs. An example is that of a public school system for all children; the Methodists encouraged governments to create this system.

Some Methodists revived Wesley's method of preaching outdoors. They called themselves The Salvation Army and took seriously God's command to help the powerless people in society. They have become well known for serving the needs of people, but their central purpose was to bring individuals to Jesus Christ.

Renewed knowledge of the Bible during the seventeenth and eighteenth centuries had its effect in various European countries. Some saw that only adults were baptized in the Bible, and believed people should be baptized only when they were able to make their own decision. Baptist Churches, Quakers, Mennonites, Moravians and other European churches developed in this way. In North America, Pentecostal, Missionary Alliance, Brethren, and other churches were formed by people attempting to follow what they believed the Bible to be saying.

In the early nineteenth century, a movement was started in America by a man named Joseph Smith. He said an angel enabled him to find metal plates and to translate markings on them into English. This was called the Book of Mormon, which cannot be examined in its original language because the metal plates are not available. Smith said the angel returned and took them away.

They established a church called The Church of Jesus Christ and Latter-day Saints, based on the Book of Mormon. Members of this movement were called Mormons. They were persecuted in the eastern United States, so they moved west and settled in Utah. From there, they sent out missionaries to convert people and established churches in Canada and other places. Their theology, based on the Book of Mormon, is very different from most of Christianity, but the spirit of Christ is evident in their way of life.

Spanish immigrants brought the Roman Catholic Church to South and Central America, where it is the principal Christian Church in that part of the world. The Roman Catholic Church continues to be the largest Christian denomination in that area and in the southern parts of Europe.

During the late nineteenth century, churches in Europe and North America sent missionaries to Africa, China, and other places to convert people to Christianity. They started Christian churches there and brought western medical care and education to the local people. Through time, African Christians came to resist European dominance in these churches. I once spoke with a black African who told me that all the leaders in the black African movement were educated in mission schools. The spirit of Christ led them to a sense of their own worth.

The Eastern Orthodox Church became the dominant Christian Church in Russia and the Ukraine. It did not have any reformation. In the twentieth century,

Communism in Russia and China suppressed Christianity, but it survived in smaller groups.

The Canadian West was settled by European people during the nineteenth century. These people brought their brands of Christianity with them. In small communities where there were scarcely enough people for one congregation, it didn't seem sensible to have several Christian churches. Local people began establishing unified Christian churches in their communities. By 1920, there were more than a thousand such union churches in Canada. Pressure mounted for unity among similar denominations in all of Canada.

The Methodist Church in Canada initiated union negotiations with other denominations. Some dropped out, but three Protestant Churches in Canada—the Methodist Church, the Congregational Church and the Presbyterian Church—came together in 1925 to become the United Church of Canada. A portion of the Presbyterian Church stayed out of the union. In 1968, a Canadian conference of the United Brethren Church in the United States joined the United Church of Canada.

Behind all denominations and theories is a deep underlying mystery that is in all life. This mystery we call God, whose nature we cannot wrap up in a tidy description or formula, can be sensed through the spirit of the life lived by Jesus of Nazareth. Giving priority to this mystery of God is the uniting factor in Christianity. Churches can unite when they make this factor more significant than their own specific style of packaging Christianity. A united Church generates an atmosphere of acceptance under God, which encourages individuals to think about their faith without fear that their conclusions will put their belonging at risk.

The United Church of Canada recognizes that others have different ways of interpreting Christianity and packaging Christianity. These ways are not only to be tolerated, but respected, although we sometimes disagree with their theories.

Church union in Canada was inspired by words in John's gospel that tell of Jesus praying *that they may all be one; even as thou, Father, art in me, and I in thee, that they also may be in us, so that the world may believe that thou hast sent me*" (John 17:21).

This quick sketch of the factors in the background of the Christian churches can help you appreciate the diversity you may find among them. Each has historical reasons for its particular style and teaching, yet all seek to express the spirit of Jesus. Each endeavours to help people relate to the mystery of God and express the love of God in their society.

I value the United Church of Canada for its spirit of encouraging people to think for themselves, while providing them with a wide variety of information and a breadth of insight, partly due to its background in several denominations.

CHAPTER NINE

Expressing Beliefs

When I first began to live with God for God, I saw that it was difficult to express the mystery of God in words. I tried to help people find a living relationship with God as revealed in Jesus, regardless of how they chose to interpret that. Learning more about the Bible and gaining additional life experience with people has led me to find that what people believe about God does make a difference.

The Catholic Church was concerned that people be unified in what they believe and produced creeds that congregations could recite together. These provide mental concepts for people to use in thinking about God. Each such creed was composed in a given time period using language and ideas that people could relate to.

An increase in knowledge and a different intellectual climate in later periods can mean that those creeds become more confusing than helpful. An example can be seen in the Apostles' Creed.

I remember the time in my teen years when, as I recited the Apostles' Creed with the congregation, for some reason I became uncomfortably aware of what I was saying. I had rambled as usual through, "I believe in God the Father Almighty, maker of heaven and earth; and in Jesus Christ his only Son our Lord, who was conceived by the Holy Ghost, born of the Virgin Mary, suffered under Pontius Pilate, was crucified, died and buried." Then I found myself saying, "He descended into hell," and stopped short.

I had been led to believe hell was a place of torment to which bad people were sent to be punished. I couldn't believe the best man who ever lived would be sent to hell. I didn't get through reciting the rest of the creed, because I was troubled about why people seemed to believe Jesus went to hell. The first chance I got, I looked up the Creed in the back of the Hymnary to examine the rest and see if it would explain why Jesus was said to go to hell.

I examined more closely the next section: "On the third day he rose again from the dead." That seemed pretty basic to the Christian faith. Then the creed said, "He ascended into heaven and sitteth on the right hand of God, the Father Almighty." I knew that ascended meant he went up. I was not nearly as sophisticated about astronomy as most young people are today, but I knew enough about planets, stars and space in general to find it confusing that Jesus was up there somewhere, sitting beside God.

I had been taught to think of Jesus as alive and present with us in life. Here the Creed said that he was off sitting beside God. Then it said, "From thence he will come to judge the quick and the dead." This obviously meant that Jesus is not with us now and when he does come in the future, he will bring judgment, not love.

As I examined the rest of the creed, it got more confusing. Next, I was being expected to affirm, "I believe in the Holy Ghost." I had been led to understand that when people imagined they saw a dead person, they called it a ghost. My parents assured me that there really is no such thing as a ghost and I shouldn't believe in ghosts. Believing in ghosts made people afraid when there was nothing to be afraid of. Here the creed expected me to say that I did believe in a ghost.

Perhaps it made a difference that this was a holy ghost, but I didn't know what holy meant. At that time, Sunday services always began with singing, "Holy, holy, holy, Lord God Almighty, early in the morning our songs shall rise to thee." Most of the congregation in that farming community had been up since 5:30 or 6:00 that morning, and it seemed unreal to be singing "early in the morning" at around 11:00. Was "holy" just as unreal? It seemed to be inserted because it had a religious ring to it.

Then the list of beliefs went on to name "the Holy Catholic Church." I knew what this meant. It meant that big church with the cross on the steeple which the people in our church seemed to feel had something wrong with it. I was apparently supposed to believe in that church.

The next line was, "the communion of saints." I had been taught that saints were people who had been very good and were considered close to God. I knew what communion was, so these words brought up a mental picture of good people sitting around eating cubes of bread and drinking red juice from little glasses.

Then I found something I could really believe in: "The forgiveness of sins." It was horrible to feel guilty and such a relief when one was forgiven.

Next, the creed said that I should believe in "the resurrection of the body." I was familiar with the term "resurrection" being used to refer to Jesus rising from the dead. Was this saying that all of us would rise in our old bodies? Most people of whose death I was aware had been pretty weak and sick the last while. When all those frail bodies were resurrected, who would look after all these sick people? It was quite a picture to think of a world full of millions and millions of old or sick people. Where would the vast numbers of people who had died over the centuries find room on the planet?

My experience is an example of how the Apostles' Creed spoke to a teenager. In recent years, more people have become conscious of what the Apostles' Creed seems to say and find it more confusing than helpful. Sufficient numbers of people do not feel comfortable declaring that they believe what it seems to be saying and many congregations have ceased to declare the Apostles' Creed.

They still feel a need for a creed which they can say together to express the historic Christian Faith, however, and several congregations sent memorials to the General Council, the national governing body of the United Church of Canada, asking that a revised version be made available for congregations. The General Council assigned this task to the standing Committee on the Christian Faith.

Dr. Donald Mather, professor of Systematic Theology at Queen's Theological College, was chairman of that committee at that time and he invited me to be one of its dozen or so members. They were theological professors from Queen's, Emanuel and McGill Universities, a past moderator of the United Church, the editor of *The Observer* (the United Church monthly publication), a few pastoral ministers, and myself among them. I welcomed the opportunity to be involved with learned people in thinking through a way for Christian faith to be expressed by a creed.

The Committee met for a full day once a month. They made several attempts to amend the Apostles' Creed, and came to the conclusion that the Apostles' Creed was an historic document which should be preserved without amendment as the thinking of its time period. They therefore obtained authority from the General Council Executive to produce a completely new creed.

The Committee on the Christian Faith worked on a new creed for two years and presented the 1966 General Council with a first draft. This was discussed at length by the Council and sent back with instructions to make some changes. After two more years of considering every phrase, the 23rd General Council in 1968 considered the second draft, which they adopted as "A New Creed."

This document had been given careful consideration phrase by phrase for one full day each month over a period of four years. It has been used not only in the United Church of Canada, but in many other Protestant denominations.

CHAPTER TEN

A New Creed

The text of this creed can be found in the 1969 United Church of Canada Service Book for the people, on page 370. It is printed here as it was approved in 1968.

Man is not alone. He lives in God's world.
We believe in God
    Who has created and is creating,
    Who has come in the true Man Jesus,
        to reconcile and make new,
Who works in us and others by his spirit.
We trust him.
He calls us to be his church,
    to celebrate his presence,
    to love and serve others,
    to seek justice and resist evil,

to proclaim Jesus, crucified and risen,
    our judge and our hope.
In life, in death, in life beyond death,
    God is with us. We are not alone,
Thanks be to God.

A revised version appears on page 918 of the United Church's *Voices United* (1994). It has also been used by other denominations and is found in their liturgical materials.

Here is "A New Creed," as revised in 1994.

We are not alone. We live in God's world.
We believe in God:
Who has created and is creating,
Who has come in Jesus, the word made flesh,
    to reconcile and make new,
Who works in us and others by the Spirit.
We trust in God.
We are called to be the church:
    to celebrate God's presence,
    to love and serve others,
    to live with respect in creation,
    to seek justice and resist evil,
    to proclaim Jesus, crucified and risen,
        our judge and our hope.
In life, in death, in life beyond death,
God is with us. We are not alone.
Thanks be to God.

"A New Creed," in its original form from 1968, is the best example in print of what I believe about Christianity. I participated in the very careful consideration that designed it and appreciate the reasons behind the wording, so I will use it as a pattern to discuss Christian beliefs.

MAN IS NOT ALONE—HE LIVES IN GOD'S WORLD

This declares in one short sentence that human beings are not the only spiritual entities with a mystery we call "I" in charge. There is a mystery behind all of life that we call God, and God is with every human being on the planet.

Religion based on the life and teaching of Jesus holds the belief that all human beings live in a world that is God's, just as a child lives in a world that belongs to his or her parents. The child knows this without attempting to define what it means. The child does not invent its father or mother; it just arrives in its parents' world. The relationship exists before any attempt to think it through or express it in words.

The child may go through many stages during which the way he or she thinks about a parent may change. This thinking may make a difference in the quality of the relationship each child has with their parent, but that relationship is always there. The child is not alone and needs constant reassurance that this is the case. This relationship of child with parent is an insightful metaphor for human relationship with God.

These opening words set the tone for everything said in the creed. God cares for each person no matter what she or he thinks or believes. Each person is not alone, whether or not they are aware of it, or can appreciate or express it. God is with you in every situation you face and with every human being you encounter. This is why our western culture, which has a heritage of Christianity, assumes every human life is sacred.

Jesus went to his hometown and spoke in the synagogue. The people warmed to him as one of their own. He was considered as belonging, until he drew attention to scriptural accounts, which showed, *"There were many widows in the land of Israel in the days of Elijah... and Elijah was sent to none of them but only to Zarephath, in the land of Sidon, to a woman who was a widow.; and there were many lepers in Israel in the time of the prophet Elisha; and none of them was cleansed, but only Na'aman the Assyrian"* (Luke 4:25–27).

When he said this, their mood changed! Suggesting God cared about foreigners was so unacceptable that they rose up in wrath and threw him out of the synagogue. It was written in Deuteronomy 7:6–7, *"You are a people holy to the Lord your God; the Lord your God has chosen you to be a people for his own... out of all the peoples that are on the earth... the Lord has set his love upon you and chose you."* They took this very literally, but Jesus had a broader understanding.

Jesus was unique in that his life and teaching revealed God as loving all people. Jesus said, *"Truly, I say to you, as you did it to one of the least of these my brethren, you did it to me"* (Matthew 25:40). Jesus went from place to place, teaching by words and actions that God cares for everybody, whatever they believe and whether or not they deserve to be loved. This is distinctive about Jesus Christ. He said we should love our enemies, because God cares about them. This drew hostility from those who believed God cared exclusively for their kind of people.

In saying that man is not alone, the creed used the term "man" as is common in English literature, to refer to humans of every gender. No one is left out when we make statements such as "Wherever man has trod," "manmade substance," "man the lifeboats," etc. By using "man" in this context, the creed declares that the whole human race is not alone, whether or not they are aware of it or have their own ways of thinking about it.

This point is significant, because belief that God cares about every human being tends to moderate the way power is used. People who believe God cares only for our people can take this as license to be ruthless with people beyond our circle. A creed that begins with "The human race is not alone" affirms a basic premise of Jesus Christ.

I was disappointed that a General Council of the United Church of Canada in 1980 removed this important element from the creed by changing it to read, "We are not alone." Something very important was lost in the change.

In interpersonal discourse, "we" is used to convey the warmth of identifying with each other. In a larger context, "we" is used of people engaged in some activity together, or a larger number who have the same race, background, interests or beliefs. It always draws a circle that distinguishes us from the rest.

To begin the creed with the term "we" implies that this statement applies to our type of people and implies that we are the only part of the human race that matters. This is the attitude Jesus challenged and is contrary to his spirit.

The feminist movement felt that due recognition of the place of women called for the English language to stop using the word "man" as inclusive of all humans. The General Council felt that a Christian church should support the feminist aspirations and the United Church of Canada recognized the significance of their concerns by eliminating the word "man" from their creed.

However commendable this intention, the Council should have taken steps to find an appropriate substitute for the word "man" that would maintain this important declaration about the whole human race. They simply accepted a quick solution.

WE BELIEVE IN GOD

At this point, the word "we" is appropriate. It would change the whole meaning to say "man believes in God," because mankind does not all believe what we go on to say about God. "We" and "man" obviously do not have the same meaning.

The Apostles' Creed begins with "I believe." In a contemporary congregation, there may be people who are uncertain about what they believe, but wish to identify with this believing community. They may not feel sincere saying "I believe," but can affirm "we believe" as a way of identifying with the congregations who believe these things.

A creed is designed to help such people know a belonging that helps them sort out what they can believe. I came to know God through feeling a belonging with God's people before I knew what I could believe.

Christians believe specific things about God, so the creed goes on to say:

GOD, WHO HAS CREATED AND IS CREATING

All Christians believe this is God's world because God created it. Creating anything begins with conceiving the idea and planning its organization. John's Gospel put it like this: *"In the beginning was the Word… without him nothing was made that was made"* (John 1:1).

The English "word" is a translation of the Greek *logos*. Logos means focused and orderly thinking. It is the root of our word logic and used for serious thinking about any subject. We use it in terms such as geology, biology, theology, criminology, paleontology, archeology, etc. Christianity affirms that without God's organized thought process conceiving the idea, and without God's decision to create it, nothing would have come into being.

The same concept is stated in Genesis 1; where the Greek used *logos*, the Hebrews expressed God's thinking process by the concept of God's speaking. God said, "Let there be light," and there was light. There was no shape or order to anything until God got the idea of a created world. God's intention, expressed through speech, brought order and purpose that resulted in a unique planet. Scientific exploration has not found anything else in the universe that approximates the amazing organization to be found in the planet earth.

Genesis 1 begins with water and outlines the stages of creation in a timeframe of six days, with humans created on the last day. For a long time, Christians believed this account was accurate in all details.

They were ignoring the other creation story, starting in Genesis 2:4. This creation story begins with nothing until it rained, so the earth was apparently composed in a desert environment. This one was oral tradition from a much earlier period, using the knowledge available at that time. It was composed several centuries before Genesis 1 and is told in narrative form because stories can hold the hearer's interest and be memorized to hand down by word of mouth to the next generation.

It tells of God creating a man. The Hebrew word used this time meant the male. It goes on to tell of God planting a garden and charging the man to till and keep it (be responsible for the environment given him). God grew plants and trees, formed animals and, last of all, a woman. This creation story does not have a six-day time schedule.

The Genesis 1 account was composed centuries later. By that time, writing was available to preserve it in a non-narrative form. In the intervening centuries, people had come to know much more about the vastness of the seas and the probable sequence of the appearance of plants and animals. Human thinking had advanced and it says that God created man, male and female. This account used the Hebrew word that meant human beings. Hebrew had a word for the specific male human that was different from the word for the whole human race. It was translation into English that combined both words into the one term "man."

The timespan between them caused the two creation accounts to differ in details, but both used the knowledge they had available to affirm that everything one sees or discovers is the way it is because of God's decision. Both stories make the same point that God created the world.

In relating to God, we are relating to the mysterious reality behind all things. This remains constant, while scientific theories are developed and changed through the emergence of new discoveries.

Scientists who develop knowledge through the order they see in the universe demonstrate that the human mind can think the way the creator thought in creating it all. Genesis 1:27 puts this as *"God created man in his own image."* Whatever science discovers, including the development of animal species over long periods that we call evolution, is part of the creative thinking of God. The creed puts it as *"God has created and is creating."*

God can be sensed in nature and can be felt working within the human soul. Christians believe that God can be known through the spirit expressed in the life and teachings of Jesus of Nazareth. This threefold awareness of God is behind the Church's teaching of the Holy Trinity, which is not a mathematical formula but rather points to ways in which the mystery of God can be sensed. This Trinitarian form can be seen in the new creed and appreciated in human experience of God.

GOD, WHO HAS COME IN THE TRUE MAN JESUS

Jesus Christ is central to Christianity. The Christian Faith Committee felt the creed should avoid any theological jargon that might not be familiar to those with little background in theology.

"The word made flesh" is a biblical expression and comes from John 1:14: *"The word became flesh and dwelt among us."* This is a way of saying that the *logos* of God lived in a real person and knowing that person has helped people to know God.

The gospel stories combine memories of what Jesus did and said and the Christian community's thinking about the mystery of his effect on people. Theories about Jesus are too often attempts to fit mystery into a firm definition that can be known objectively. The mystery of God, like the mystery another person thinks of as "I", can be known through personal relationship rather than through definition.

Did you ever try to describe what you mean by "I"

and have trouble finding words that define it as you, distinct from the general meaning of those words that could apply to many people? Only you really know the mystery you mean by "I", and only God knows the mystery we mean when we use the word God. God knows the mystery you call "I". He made it.

Rather than try to explain God's internal makeup, which we cannot really know, it makes more sense to recognize that God, who can be experienced in nature or within ourselves, is the God who came into human history in the form of Jesus. Colossians 1:19 says of Jesus, *"In him all the fullness of God was pleased to dwell"* The new creed doesn't say "God who is Jesus," but "God who comes in Jesus." This is not a precise definition, but a better way to point to a mystery.

TO RECONCILE AND MAKE NEW

We can know a personal relationship with God as seen in Jesus. We can know God's care and intention for people through observation of what Jesus said and did. We can sense the vitality of a living God by sensing that living spirit in Jesus. God is not a philosophical conclusion, but is alive as Jesus was alive. *"If anyone is in Christ, he is a new creation; the old has passed away, the new has come"* (2 Corinthians 5:17). The new creed put it: "to reconcile and make new." What I call living with God for God brings a sense of newness to life.

GOD, WHO WORKS IN US AND OTHERS BY HIS SPIRIT

Spirit is a concept not easily described, but we know what it is to be captured by a spirit in a crowd, or even alone. We use the term Spirit to refer to that mystery which can take hold of people and inspire them to be and do more than they normally would. A generous spirit can move us to help, but a vengeful spirit can move a crowd to do cruel things.

The 1980 revision removed the possessive pronoun "his," which was vitally important because God works in us by Jesus' spirit, not simply by "the" spirit. Mobs generate spirit, as do hockey games. Any number of spirits could be meant by "the" spirit. When Jesus spoke to the synagogue in his home community, he said, *"The spirit of The Lord is upon me"* (Luke 4:18). He did not say, "The spirit is upon me."

People in biblical times considered God too awesome to speak directly to ordinary mortals. They spoke of God communicating through his messenger (*angelos*) or his spirit. The Bible says that it was through an angel that God told Joseph and Mary about Jesus' birth and announced it to shepherds.

God's spirit is spoken of as descending on Jesus at his baptism like a dove, and upon the first Christians at Pentecost like wind and fire. In John 3:5–8, Jesus compares spirit to wind. The Hebrew word for spirit is the same as for breath or wind.

When I was a child, I thought that a wind was air blowing right here. Much later, I learned that air moving from one place to another over vast areas is experienced locally as wind. To put it another way, wind in your street or field is not just a local phenomenon. It is the local manifestation of movement in a large portion of the atmosphere. Holy Spirit is the local manifestation of God who is everywhere.

I believe that Holy Spirit is not a separate entity, but a way of referring to God being felt in a given situation. God did not tell Moses, "My spirit will be with you," but *"I will be with you"* (Genesis 26:3). God works by making his presence felt in people.

In John 4:24, Jesus says, *"God is spirit."* That spirit working in us is God present and active, who works *"in us and others by his spirit."* I believe this is a helpful way to describe what is essentially a mystery.

WE TRUST HIM

Trust does not mean believing that God will change things to suit me if I say the right prayers. Such an approach assumes that what matters is me getting my way and using God as my agent. Manipulating God is the opposite of trusting.

Trusting is letting go of control. God is God, and I'm not. Trust means leaving the outcome to God without needing to see a blueprint of how everything will work out. Believing in God is like wading in a lake and getting your feet wet. Trusting God is like jumping in and finding that the water holds you up. A little bit of Christianity has a little bit of effect. It is in trusting your whole self to God that you can experience your soul being "made new."

HE CALLS US TO BE HIS CHURCH

A call is not a command. It leaves the hearer free to make a decision whether or not to respond. I use the "he" and "his" words of the original creed of 1968, because what is meant here is a personal call. To say "we" are called is passive and leaves the source of the call quite vague. If I am called by the clock to begin something, it is quite different than if a friend calls me to do something with him or her. In the latter case, I respond in terms of my relationship with the caller. I can be completely objective with the clock, but if I ignore a friend's call, this indicates that the friend doesn't matter much to me. If my relationship to God has depth, it will lead me to become involved in a church.

This call is not to any one specific church, but to some organized group of people who gather together regularly for Christian worship and to share in what they may do to serve God.

I would not attempt to say which church would be best for you. The decision is up to you, but I offer a number of standards I would use in selecting a church.

1. A church that nourishes relationship with the mystery of God.
2. A church that does not box God in by

claiming to be the only church God
will accept.

3. A church that exposes me to the great
    thoughts that have been preserved in
    the Bible, but seeks the spirit of Christ
    without limiting it to the exact written
    words.

4. A church that encourages me to think
    and grow in my understanding of the
    spirit of Christ revealed in Jesus.

5. A church that helps me to be aware
    of what is going on in the world and
    encourages me to think wisely about
    what I can do to help.

6. A church that inspires me with vision
    of what might be accomplished for the
    kingdom of God and encourages me to
    make whatever contribution I may be
    able to make.

However, I may not find a congregation that has all
these attributes, in which case I should accept responsibility to help the congregation that is available become
more effective in these areas. A local church is the place
where Christianity is visible. The ongoing life of a congregation brings faith into contact with human realities.

TO CELEBRATE HIS PRESENCE

The church lives in its weekly gatherings. "A New
Creed" says this is a time to celebrate that God is with

us. What form this takes will be influenced by what has happened in the history of that denomination, but the Lord's Supper will be included.

The bread may be pieces broken from one loaf. It may be pre-cut in small cubes or it may be given as unleavened wafers. The wine may be fermented grape juice (alcoholic) from a common chalice or it may be non-alcoholic grape juice in individual glasses.

Some churches may teach that these elements have been changed in substance to become the real body and blood of Jesus Christ. In others, the elements are seen as symbolic.

Despite the apparent differences, all worshipers can enter by this sacrament into the mystery of the spirit of Jesus.

In most churches, this sacrament is presided over by an ordained person to indicate that this is an action of the whole Christian Church. Ordination does not mean this person has some sort of magic, or that he or she can do it more effectively than others; ordination simply designates a role of representing the Christian Church in any and every situation. Having an ordained person presiding over the sacrament helps each participant to identify both with being part of Jesus' Church as well as being a disciple of Jesus. This sacrament is a special celebration to set the tone and spirit for each week's celebration and for all the church does to nourish dimensions of the soul.

In the first dimension, a Christian congregation can encourage its members to be thankful to God for the opportunity and resources to obtain their needs and stimulate generosity to contribute to the needs of others.

A congregation can minister to the dimension of belonging by ensuring that each person is made to feel welcome and recognized by name. The reality of each person feeling loved and accepted expresses the sacred value of each human life belonging with God.

A congregation can expand the dimension of knowledge through teaching, sermons and study groups. Insight into what has happened in the past can help one find wisdom for living in the present. It should stimulate thinking that expands understanding and seeks wisdom.

A congregation should entrust each member with some area of responsibility, to give practice in small matters that can fit the soul for responsibility in larger matters.

A congregation should have a vision of what it proposes to accomplish. It should promote causes that serve human needs in order to expand the vision dimension of its members.

A congregation should consistently uphold moral and ethical living by teaching and example. Sometimes the pressure of events, and too often self-interest, tempt people to do things that can be damaging to others. Belonging with a church congregation can be an influence that keeps one aware of belonging with God and encourages resistance to temptation.

A congregation ministers to the seventh dimension, love, by being a place where people can feel the love of God in the other members and share compassion for people beyond this fellowship. It practices love for each other that each may love all persons.

The congregation observes Sunday as holy so that each individual may find holiness every day.

An act of worship may be entertaining, but it should not be intended as a show. To worship is to participate rather than to spectate. To be in church as a mere spectator may mean missing the dynamics of mystery.

Much of what goes on in worship depends upon the "I" of each individual participant. If you bring to worship an intention to be open to the spirit, the experience enables you to receive a message from God.

Some individuals have been touched by the presence of God through certain styles of music, rituals or words. Others may find a different style helpful for them. To worship together in ways that meet the needs of several different types of people is challenging. Worshiping together calls us to care about the needs of each person, more than our own comfort with familiar patterns.

Celebration of God's presence together with one another can help each of us to be more of what God created us to be. There is a mystery here that brings the influence of God into each of the dimensions of the soul. This is not mechanical or chemical, but a dynamic mystery that happens when we are engaged in being the church in this place. It leads us to sense God's call to other responsibilities.

TO LIVE WITH RESPECT IN CREATION

This section was added in 1994 in response to something that was happening in society. Many of the original people on this continent believed that God expected people to treat all of nature with respect. In recent years, we have come to listen to the wisdom of First Nations people, and learn from their insights. This wisdom harmonized with our growing awareness of the need to care for the environment. These factors influenced the General Council of the United Church of Canada to add this line to "A New Creed."

The Bible was written in a time when the resources of nature seemed unlimited. Respect for creation got little mention, except in Genesis 2:15: *"The Lord God took the man and put him in the Garden of Eden to till it and keep it."* Caring for the garden God has given us is a serious issue now that the human race has multiplied and there are so many people using the planet's resources. This challenge is complicated by a multitude of factors. Christianity does not have a tidy formula for caring for the earth. It calls us to live with respect for creation and use human ingenuity to work out how best to go about it.

TO LOVE AND SERVE OTHERS

Jesus reveals God as having compassionate love for all people and calls us to love each other. Our interactions with every person should be in ways that are for his or her good. We instinctively love our children, but it takes a more generous spirit to love our brothers or sisters and those in our particular group. It takes even more to love strangers we scarcely know and may not even like. To find this extra love, we need to feel enfolded in the love of God, who also loves each of those persons.

Love is a distinctive essence in Christianity.

The first epistle of John says, *"He who says he is in the light and hates his brother is in the darkness still"* (1 John 2:9), and *"This is the message which you have heard from the beginning, that we should love one another"* (1 John 3:11).

John's epistle says that love is proof of new life: *"We know that we have passed out of death into life, because we love"* (1 John 3:14). No man has ever seen God; if we love one another, God abides in us and his love is expressed through us. Christianity expands the dimension of love and becomes the love of God living through your soul, loving people because God loves them.

Jesus teaches, *"I say to you, love your enemies and pray for those who persecute you"* (Matthew 5:44). This does not come naturally. It seems more natural to hate those we identify as our enemies. Being able to love with compassion unconditionally is a gift that comes through a relationship with God in Jesus. Jesus said of his followers, *"You will know them by their fruits"* (Matthew 7:16). The first of these fruits is love.

Living with God, and sensing God's presence in us, is at the heart of being the church. Living with God bears the fruit of being enabled to love with God's compassion and brings joy, peace, patience, kindness, goodness, gentleness and self-control into the soul (Galatians 5:22).

Using our skills, resources and efforts to do something for people in need can often make a great difference in their ability to deal with their immediate problems. The goal of compassionate love is to encourage people to strengthen their capacity to make life work without our help.

The local congregation can become a place for us to practice loving and encouraging ordinary persons. This includes forgiving one another when we fail. It offers a setting in which we can share in seeking understanding of what we can do to help. This help may come in the form of small ways that may seem to bring little results, but every act of service is a significant part of God's purpose. As Jesus put it, *"Truly, I say to you, as you did it to one of the least of these my brethren, you did it to me"* (Matthew 25:40).

The cumulative effect can be much more than we know. Think of the culture around us in this country and notice the effects of centuries of Christian influence. We have schools to develop the minds of children, and hospitals and many agencies to look after the sick.

Organizations spring up to involve volunteers helping people in various sorts of trouble. We become so accustomed to these things that we seldom recognize that the few who do the work to make these things happen have caught the spirit of Jesus. The majority who support their efforts are people who for many years have been exposed to the spirit of Jesus.

SEEK JUSTICE AND RESIST EVIL

For many people, the word justice seems to have the connotation of being sure that the ones who do wrong get adequately punished. Christianity sees justice as everyone getting treated fairly. The prophets proclaimed that God's people must provide care for the powerless in concrete ways. This has been integral to Christianity, but has been too often neglected in varying degrees. In recent years a way of thinking called "liberation theology" has reminded Christians of this mandate to seek justice.

Endemic poverty is perpetuated by any system that ensures an unequal distribution of wealth. God calls us to seek ways to adjust our systems to give the less fortunate a better opportunity to share in the wealth of society. God calls us not only to generosity that helps the poor, but also to be an influence for opening up opportunities for them to better themselves.

Freedom and equality are both generally recognized as good. However, complete freedom gives the strong a free hand to exploit the weak, while complete equality can only be maintained by placing limits on what the strong may do. Christianity teaches that justice is not found in either complete freedom or complete equality, but in a balance that must be continually adjusted to share the wealth without discouraging ambition. This is a mystery which cannot be strictly imposed, but must be continually sought.

To resist evil is also dynamic. Evil is anything that hurts the sacredness of human life. It must be recognized and resisted in any human situation. God calls us to recognize the evil in an inclination, before it gets acted upon. Resisting evil is a human responsibility before God that has nothing to do with a devil. The theory of a devil simplifies the origins of evil, and dilutes responsibility to seek understanding of what is happening. I repeat, I do not believe in a devil.

Many instincts and desires that are normal and appropriate can be sought in ways that have evil in them. God does not call us to reject these instincts that God has given, but to be alert to recognize the point at which natural inclinations may turn into evil ones. God expects us to avoid going beyond that point.

I do not believe that God expects exact conformity to rules or social conventions, but he definitely condemns any actions or attitudes that result in damaging people. Living with God calls us to recognize when this happens and may call us to take decisive action to stop the damage. It also calls us to accept the guilt if we are part of wrong actions, or if we are failing to do or promote what is right.

When wrongdoing is confessed with sincere intention to not repeat it in future, the spirit of Jesus teaches that a loving God welcomes this change and forgives (remember the Prodigal Son). In Christianity, we confessing our own sins and forgive others their sins. Jesus taught us to pray, *"Forgive us our sins, for we ourselves forgive every one who is indebted to us"* (Luke 11:4). Christianity can be lived despite setbacks when we always return to God regularly. This is the reason for observing one day each week as holy. Taking time for God each Sunday is not a petty rule, but a way of staying in a living relationship with God. Neglecting this scheduled return to God can lead to drifting into patterns of life that are damaging to one's self or to others.

If a society recognizes and believes in Christian virtues, that culture's tone of life changes. Mystery deals in dynamics rather than with the precision of engineering or mathematics, but it has the power to effect significant change. Living with God for God brings you into human relationships that influence individuals and society for good.

Where the new creed says, "God calls us to seek justice and resist evil," the operative words are "seek" and "resist." Both are ongoing processes rather than quick fixes.

PROCLAIM JESUS

Proclaiming Jesus was part of the life Jesus' followers. Fifty days after Jesus was crucified and resurrected, his followers gathered together on the day of the Jewish feast of Pentecost. There, they had a unique Holy Spirit experience that gave them courage to speak out about Jesus. Peter is quoted as proclaiming: *"Let all the house of Israel therefore assuredly know that God has made him both Lord and Christ, this Jesus whom you crucified"* (Acts 2:36).

Peter addressed a crowd at the temple and proclaimed Jesus. The apostles were seized and brought before the High Priest and elders, who told them not to speak or teach at all in the name of Jesus, *"but Peter and John answered them, 'Whether it is right in the sight of God to listen to you rather than God, you must judge; for we cannot but speak of what we have seen and heard'"* (Acts 4:19–20). They never ceased teaching and preaching Jesus as the Christ either at the Temple or in the home.

That Jesus was executed by the Romans at the instigation of religious leaders and, that he came back from the dead, is believed by all Christians. Christianity expanded because followers of Jesus felt called to proclaim that Jesus, who was crucified and risen, had been sent by God and was still alive among them. His followers spoke of this new life in such terms as life more abundant, life eternal, or living in Jesus.

His death and return were crucial to their conviction that he was the one sent by God. Whatever words they used to tell what happened were attempts to point to a mystery that defies explanation. The reality was that they found in Jesus a personal loving relationship with God, coupled with a capacity to love and care for each other and all human beings. The church is called to see that these things are never forgotten.

CRUCIFIED AND RISEN

Numerous writers have struggled to reconcile the crucifixion with the theory that God has willed everything that happens. The obvious answer is that this theory must be rethought. The definition of evil is that it is against the will of God, and therefore it is contradictory to suggest that God planned the evil.

Teaching that God sent Jesus to die as a sacrifice or a substitute to pay God for our sins has been considered by many to be an integral part of Christian doctrine. However, it portrays God as subject to some higher authority, such that God had to devise a horribly unjust scheme to get around this limitation. I cannot believe God is limited in this way, or that God would be party to what was evil.

I believe God's purpose for Jesus was to demonstrate God's love and inspire people to live that love in their relationships with one another. God did not plan Jesus' crucifixion. It was the result of an evil conspiracy, but God's power over evil was demonstrated by Jesus' resurrection. The gospel is the good news that God is like we see him in Jesus, triumphing over evil. His return from death inspired his followers. The cross is the universal symbol of all Christianity.

OUR JUDGE

John 12:47 quotes Jesus as saying, *"If any one hears my sayings and does not keep them, I do not judge him, for I did not come to judge the world but to save the world."* Jesus rejects the idea of being a judge, as in a court of law, who pronounces sentences. Jesus is a living presence who challenges us.

Jesus Christ sets a standard in human life, and as human beings we must continually be judged by how well we measure up to Christ. Christianity holds up that standard, not as a hurdle we must jump, but as a goal we reach for.

OUR HOPE

Hope has always been an element in the faith of God's people. It first focused on the Israelites gaining freedom from slavery in Egypt. In the wilderness, their hope focused on a promised land. In exile, their hope focused on returning to the homeland. When occupied by a foreign power, they found that Persian religion offered hope for heaven in a life beyond this one. In times of tribulation, they hoped for a Messiah, a king who would free the nation and see that God's will would be done in this lifetime.

Jesus brought hope for the kingdom of God, when all people, not just his nation, would do the will of God. Jesus' coming back from death inspires faith that evil cannot kill that hope, and that death does not defeat God.

IN LIFE, IN DEATH AND IN LIFE BEYOND DEATH, GOD IS WITH US

There is a message in one of the best-known parts of the Bible that touches a chord in the human soul. Psalm 23 uses a common occupation, the shepherd tending sheep, to speak of the mystery of God.

The teamster puts a bit in the horse's mouth and controls it with reins. The cow herder carries a stick to control the cattle. However, the shepherd of that day didn't use reins for control or a stick to hit his animals. He went in front and led the sheep. They followed him because they trusted him. God does not control people with reins or drive them with a stick. God leads and his people follow because they trust him.

There are many powerful images in this psalm. One of the most remembered passages is: *"Even though I walk through the valley of the shadow of death, I will fear no evil for thou art with me, thy rod and thy staff, they comfort me"* (Psalm 23:4). The shepherd of that day carried a short club (a rod) to fight off wild animals that might injure the sheep and a long staff to guide the sheep. The staff had a hook at the end to retrieve a lamb or sheep that was unable to get out of a narrow place. The psalm expressed faith that God will guard, like the shepherd's rod, and guide or save, like the shepherd's staff.

All of us will have to walk through the valley of the shadow of death, the death of one we love, or our own death. The creed does not offer any description of what happens after death. Some people have used terms like gates of pearl or streets of gold. A spiritual song from the days of slavery in the United States says, "All God's children got shoes. When I get to heaven, I'm gonna put on my shoes and walk all over God's heaven." Shoes for slaves who must go barefoot, or pearls and gold for people who live in poverty, endeavour to speak of having more than one could ever have in this life.

Theories about heaven are attempts to describe a mystery that no one really understands. The apostle Paul uses the metaphor of planting a seed: *"What you sow does not come to life unless it dies. What you sow is not the body which is to be, but a bare kernel... God gives it a body as he has chosen"* (1 Corinthians 15:36–38). Careful examination of an unfamiliar seed cannot tell you what sort of plant will grow from that seed. God has designed that a plant will grow from the seed. Each plant has a life that is an enhancement of the potential in the seed.

That metaphor says to me that knowing what life is like here cannot tell us what kind of life may lie beyond death. We must leave that in God's hands.

By knowing the God of love in the spirit of Jesus, we have confidence that, as this psalm says, *"Goodness and mercy shall follow me all the days of my life; and I shall dwell in the house of the Lord forever"* (Psalm 23:6). This is expressed in the words of the new creed: "In life, in death and in life beyond death, God is with us."

Sooner or later, each of us will have to face our own death. God is with us as we face the end of this life. This is a mystery words cannot define precisely. Living with God through whatever experiences life brings gives assurance that we will be with God in the experience of death.

My faith is in God rather than in any formula about heaven. Christianity is not about knowing all the answers, but about living with God who cares, and trusting God for the future. I trust God to see me through death and take care of whatever happens next.

WE ARE NOT ALONE

"A New Creed" began with affirmation that the whole human race, including each individual, is/are not alone, even if they are not aware of it. It then speaks of the nature of this mystery we call God and what God expects of us. In the light of all this, we (in the appropriate meaning of "we") can declare our faith that we are not alone. The appropriate conclusion is, therefore, "Thanks be to God."

This creed deals with the fact that the mystery cannot be described exactly. It was designed to encourage your own best thinking about how each phrase applies. "A New Creed" provides a basic concept of God and of what it means to live for God in the spirit of Jesus Christ, without closing off further thought.

CHAPTER ELEVEN

Christianity Today

I have known many people who have been led to think that Christians must believe certain theories. They felt they could not be Christians if they were no longer able to believe those theories. I can understand, because I have been there.

I have seen these people get fresh inspiration for living by discovering, as I did, that the essential belief is in the mystery behind the whole of life that is called God and is revealed in the spirit of Jesus Christ. You can relate to God personally whether or not you believe theories that no longer make sense for you.

This relationship to God affects all seven dimensions of the soul. It generates power in the soul to deal with whatever life brings. It opens up opportunities for fullness of life now and after death. It can bring a new sense of wholeness that has been called being "born again."

This may convince some individuals that their specific church or doctrine is the only way acceptable to God. This conviction, that God accepts only our type of people with our style of worship or teaching doctrine, has been common to most primitive religions. It has been claimed by the Hebrews, the Temple in Israel, the Catholic Church, various evangelical protestant churches, as well as unusual ones like the Jehovah's Witnesses and Mormons. Of course, they cannot all be correct.

Limiting God in this way can appeal to our desire for security, but it is not in the spirit of Jesus. Jesus was thrown out of a synagogue because he taught that God loves and accepts all who sincerely turn to him! Jesus died that we might know this.

Throughout the history of God's people, theories have been developed to help people relate to the mystery of God—and others have distorted it. Expanding knowledge has led people to sort out which ones are valuable and which misleading, and each individual's thinking contributes to this process. Your own personal insights may help you find wisdom, but they are not absolute presuppositions. They must always be subject to further thought.

Christianity is not an exact science, like mathematics, but rather a dynamic mystery. The people who have been exposed to the spirit of Jesus and have made decisions in their souls that have lifted the quality of their lives have also influenced their society. The spirit of Jesus has continued to live. As John 1:5 puts it, *"The light shines in darkness, and the darkness has not overcome it."*

Christianity relates the mystery one thinks of as "I" to the mystery of God, as revealed in Jesus. Religious teachers of Jesus' day agreed with him that *"you shall love the Lord your God with all your heart, and with all your soul, and with all your mind. This is the great and first commandment. And a second is like it, You shall love your neighbor as yourself. On these two commandments depend all the law and the prophets"* (Matthew 22:37–40). Such love is mystery, and throughout life the mystery is what matters.

Jesus, by the spirit of his life and teaching, reveals God as loving all people. That love seeks a responding love from us that brings to our relationship with God all the emotional fervour we symbolize by the heart, all the values and decisions we make in our souls, all the wisdom of our best thinking in our minds, and then gives these concrete expression by using our strength, energy and abilities in serving other people. This I call living with God for God.

Living with God for God is guided by the principles of the Ten Commandments and the teaching and example of Jesus, but these must be interpreted in the spirit of Jesus. This gets worked out amidst the pressures and possibilities of contemporary life through regular worship with others and constantly relating in prayer to the mystery of God.

This is Christianity as I understand it. I have tried to communicate this with words, but words can only speak to your mind. It is when the mystery of your "I" enters a relationship with the mystery behind all life, known through the spirit of Christ, that these things become real for you. May you find wholeness in your soul through living with God for God in a loving relationship that continues into eternity.

You are not alone!

About the Author

The United Church of Canada ordained George Richardson as a Christian minister in 1960. He served several small rural charges and then for twenty-two years he ministered a congregation of more than 600 families at St. Paul's United Church in Perth, Ontario.

George's original calling in life was to farm. He tells the story in this book of that calling taking a turn, which meant leaving the farm at age thirty to take the education he had missed in his teen years, in order to meet the requirements for ministry.

George served as minister in local congregations and also in national and district responsibility, including Presbytery Chairman and Conference President. He represented his conference on the General Council

Executive for five years where his contribution brought him a nomination for Moderator of the United Church of Canada in 1986.

George served on numerous national committees that brought together informed persons from all across Canada to research matters of Christian concern and consider together what to recommend to the church's top court. Meeting in these committees monthly exposed George to the focused thinking of intelligent persons from all across Canada.

George shared in the Christian Faith Committee's work that produced a statement which enabled persons to state together their Christian faith in plain language designed for use in Sunday worship. This was approved by the General Council in 1968 and called A New Creed.

George Richardson writes out of many years of personal pastoral experience with all sorts of people in many insightful situations.

He may be contacted via email: geoeun@bell.net.